The Irish Literary Revival

Its History, Pioneers and Possibilities

By
William Patrick Ryan

LEMMA PUBLISHING CORPORATION
NEW YORK
1970

THE IRISH LITERARY REVIVAL

A Lemma Publishing Corporation Reprint Edition

This Lemma Publishing Corporation edition of
William Patrick Ryan's *The Irish Literary Revival*
is an unabridged republication of the first edition
published in London in 1894.

International Standard Book Number 0-87696-004-2
Library of Congress Catalog Card Number 78-110293

Published by
Lemma Publishing Corporation
509 Fifth Avenue
New York, N.Y. 10017

For sale and distribution only in the United States.

Printed in U.S.A.

THE IRISH LITERARY REVIVAL:

Its History, Pioneers and Possibilities.

WITH PORTRAITS

BY W. P. RYAN.

Author of "The Heart of Tipperary: a Romance."

PUBLISHED BY THE AUTHOR

AT

1, CONSTANCE ROAD, EAST DULWICH, LONDON. S.E.

1894.

PATERNOSTER STEAM PRESS,
IVY LANE, LONDON, E.C.; AND FROME.

PREFACE.

HIS little book is, in the first place, a record of Irish literary awakenings and endeavours during the past ten years. The Irish literary movement, of which so much has been heard of late, has now passed its decade. In the stress and tension of Irish political interests it remained too long unnoted in the background. It is now of national importance, great in its possibilities of good for Ireland, and, mayhap, not without promise of wider influence.

As the movement has the adhesion of nearly every Irish writer and scholar of the period, this book must needs be in some degree a study of the Irish *littèrateurs* of our time. Of late the movement has attracted a large share of attention, and it cannot be an unnecessary labour to show the personalities and purposes of those who have moulded and are moulding it.

I have said in the volume itself that literary Ireland consists of many fragments, very far apart and very strange to one another. Even our leading literary societies, working for the same purposes, are not yet like the wings or sections of the same organisation. Literary Ireland in fact does not know itself. Hence not only have I to show what our several workers are like, but I have to try, so to speak, to introduce a great many of them to one another, hoping through all that the task may tend in some measure to that cohesion and fraternity without which a movement is, to a large extent, ineffectual.

It were easy to prolong this volume to much greater length. However, such elaborate treatment may well wait over for a time when finer achievements are to be chronicled. I find our Irish reapers eager at their early tasks, singing their morning songs, so to speak, in the golden corn-fields ; a few old reapers looking on and blessing the work. I find them, for the most part, a merry and a Celtic company, and I would wish that others should come to see and hear them too. The historian who will come when the work is done and the harvest gathered, will have far greater results than I to chronicle ; but will he not miss much of the happy enthusiasm, the gaily-going life of the morning and the forenoon ? The great Reaper will have gathered some of our reapers to himself. There will be fewer songs and more shadows.

It is my pleasant duty to make special acknowledgment of my thanks to leaders in the London, Dublin, and provincial Irish Literary Societies for the cordial enthusiasm and sympathy with which they hailed this venture.

W. P. RYAN.

London, *March, 1894.*

CONTENTS.

The Irish Literary Revival.

I.

INTRODUCTORY.

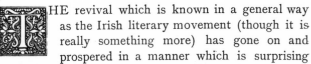HE revival which is known in a general way as the Irish literary movement (though it is really something more) has gone on and prospered in a manner which is surprising even to the Irish students and thinkers who, a decade ago, were dreaming what to others seemed the vain dream of an Irish Renaissance. Hopeful and thoughtful they stood, but in their then far-divided centres, like the palm they stood in a realm of sand. A time has come when, if the land of promise is not really in sight, the desert sands are passed, the balm and the harvests of new climes have been felt and seen. In truth, this movement has developed much faster than the hopes of some of its originators, and a possible danger is that they will unconsciously fail to keep pace with it. To show that they cannot afford to stand still or to be dilatory is no needless task.

We have had some studies of the movement, more or

less from the outside, and looked at chiefly in its recent
developments. I purpose to review it from an inner
and independent standpoint, and to trace it as it ought
to be traced—from the beginning. In two addresses
the president of the Irish Literary Society, London, has
surveyed its ethical and national aspect. The Rev.
Stopford Brooke has dealt with one important side of
its intellectual mission; Dr. Sigerson, Dr. Hyde, and
other critics have furnished other side-lights and points.
No study as yet has surveyed the movement as a
whole, has taken cognisance of the several schools
within it, has recognised how much wider it is than
the rallying-grounds of the existing literary societies,
how really racy of the soil it is, how typical of certain
Irish qualities, and how gradually its roots have
grown from various elements of Celtic Ireland. In an
age of personal journalism its promoters have not,
with few exceptions, received due note. A few prominent personages, more or less in its inner councils, have
been shadowed by the amiable gossips of the personal
press, who, needless to say, have seen or noted little of
the intellectual personalities of their subjects. Irishmen
have need and reason to pursue the study with eyes
that will see deeper. If in the movement there is real
propagandism, anything lofty, or likely to endure, the
lives and life-work of its promoters will suggest it. I
do not think that the significance of the movement is
fully realised in the outside world, the courses into
which it has branched, the enthusiasm it has kindled in
far-out places. I believe that within it there are men
with missions which ought to be memorable, as well as
men whose best work, perhaps, has been done, work

which belongs to another era and another school; men also who, though they figure in its councils and serve it faithfully, are not wholly aware of its actual trend. A study of this kind can hardly justify itself unless it can clearly illustrate and differentiate what are the moving forces and what the forces moved; what is the spirit, and what galvanic or ephemeral interest. The movement has not been so sudden a growth as some critics imagine. The causes that have contributed to its rise are many. After efforts sometimes crude and obscure it has found light and the highway. Great is the hope that is bound up with it ; fruitful are the fields wherein it has set young workers working. It ought to appeal, in some degree, to all who ponder upon Irish problems, and look to the heart of Irish needs ; for its guides—or at least many of them—have generous national and social ideals before them, as well as their essentially intellectual ones. Those who are not prepared for this fact do not realise the striking way in which life, love of culture, literature, and scholastic enthusiasm are bound up in the Gaelic nature when at its best. Perhaps with the expansion and success of this revival—always remembering the educational and social, as well as the purely literary aims of it—the destinies of things Irish are more closely identified than many political students imagine. It is the visible evidence of that critical, studious Ireland which has been gathering itself to itself, and finding its strength behind the social changes and the political scene-shifting of the past few years. There are some despairful and confusing elements in the Irish life of our time, there are social wrecks and ruins which it were folly to ignore ; but those who imagine on that

account that the country is lapsing to decay or chaos
are superficial observers. They study the rags she is
casting off, not the new garb. They have little insight
into the unchanging traits of Irish life, none at all
into that spiritual Ireland which is too sensitive to find
satisfying life even in the highest form of politics. An
active section in this new intellectual force was inspired
and moulded by the Land League, as these pages cannot avoid showing. Others deemed the League but cloud
and darkness; others again saw in it mingled good and
evil. Their junction has been productive of new views,
and mutual good for their critical spirit and judgment.
They have discovered a common national ground,
haunted by faery music, and made sacred by common
human traditions. They have many missions before
them. One aim is to turn the minds of the scattered
sections of the Irish people more intently to the realisation of their Celtic selves, without which knowledge
they may only lead stunted lives. Dr. Douglas Hyde's
lecture on " The Necessity of De-Anglicising the Irish
Nation," * was a startling revelation of the extent to
which we had aped foreign fashions, of a nature the least
suited to our character and requirements. It was a
diagnosis of one of our worst diseases, one which would
make either literary or national revolutions impossible.
A second aim is largely educational. This is as it
should be, for the Irish people are by nature a literary
and educating people. Culture and intellectual gain
have been guiding thoughts with them whenever their
energies have had a fair field. The idea of culture and

* Delivered at the Dublin National Literary Society, November
25th, 1892.

education was inwoven with the life and thought of the Gaelic period. The bards and brehons were learned institutions in themselves. Cormac MacArt, more than fifteen centuries ago, founded three great schools, quite national in their character, in Ireland; and an old chronicler says with Celtic enthusiasm: "The world was full of beauty and goodness in his time." After Ireland's conversion to Christianity her schools became famous, her sons were missionaries and educational enthusiasts abroad. In the Danish period a frequent cause of popular wrath was the invaders' demolition of the people's literature. The stringent Penal Laws directed against education prove its force in later times. Later still the "poor scholars" were almost an institution in Ireland. They were characteristic of herself and her story. In their misery and their love for knowledge they were typical at once of her political fall, her intellectual faith and strength. In our days, in the quiet villages and the lonely country reaches, learning is reverenced as something far above the run of mere worldly things. The peasant's inherent regard for the "ould stock," the fairy kingdom and ghost-land, is a simple force beside his reverence for scholarship. The spirit is there, dim too often, always capable of expansion. Still by Irish fields and Irish firesides, there is the *grah* for the old lore and legends. There is yet a Fata Morgana of wonderful lights and traditions upon the mountain heights above the Irish peasant. Realising this inborn love of the Celt for knowledge and lore of so many kinds, it is no wonder that there should be to-day a band of Irishmen whose first purpose is to convince their brethren that devotion to those scholastic and

literary ideals is the surest sign of their being true to
themselves ; that Ireland has need of men who would
be apostles of study and culture, as essentially as Father
Mathew was an apostle of temperance.   This is one of
the most salient ideas in the new departure, and it is
amongst its most hopeful ones.   It is not, of course,
directly concerned with the creation of literature, but it
is one of the fine forces which will make a real Irish
literature possible.

   Another section in the movement, whose personalities
we can study in the pages that follow, is one of literary
enthusiasts, pure and simple ; some whose natures and
intellects are Celtic to a fault ; who would have Ireland's
literature really expressive of herself ; a literature
through which an Irish voice would sound as truly as
through the Irish melodies themselves—sometimes sad
with the emigrant's parting cry, sometimes weird with
the fairy-call from the rath—others who plan a literature
which will have no land as its home, will be wide as
humanity, leaving us like Love in Mr. Yeats' poem,

> " To pace upon the mountains far above,
> And hide his head amid a crowd of stars."

The thought of an Irish Renaissance, after all the
pathos, seething life, and seeming chaos of ten centuries,
reminds me of a few touching words in the prelude to
George Eliot's " Middlemarch " : — " Many Theresas
have been born who found for themselves no epic life
wherein there was a constant unfolding of far-resonant
action ; perhaps only a life of mistakes, the offspring of
a certain spiritual grandeur ill-matched with the mean-
ness of opportunity ; perhaps only a tragic failure which

found no sacred poet, and sank unwept into oblivion. With dim lights and tangled circumstances, they tried to shape their thought and deed in noble agreement; but, after all, to common eyes their struggles seemed mere inconsistency and formlessness." Has it not been so with the Celt? His story, rightly studied, shows his years to be a long yearning for that epic life; but the battle-field, the scaffold, the famine grave, or the emigrant coffin-ship, have too often been the rude results, the end, the burial-places of his spiritual grandeur. But a glorious revenge were his if, in an era when peace and the fruition of his national hopes had found him, gifted children should arise and interpret that epic soul to the world.

Such interpreters we have now to meet. How far they have already succeeded, and how far it may be possible for them yet to succeed in their mission of interpretation, we shall see and judge.

II.

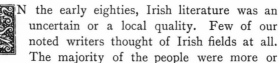

N the early eighties, Irish literature was an uncertain or a local quality. Few of our noted writers thought of Irish fields at all. The majority of the people were more or less pre-occupied with an intense political struggle. Literary levers were here and there brought into force in the Land League period, but only a few writers won anything like fame for Irish work. William O'Brien was as yet only a militant journalist, voicing the fever of his time as earnestly as Davis did the enthusiasm of '42, or Mitchel the passion of '48. The late Miss Rose Kavanagh furnished studies of a simple, idyllic Ulster life, of a kind which certain political utterances would never lead us to expect in the northern province. In "The Wild Birds of Killeevy," Miss Rosa Mulholland gave us a memorable idyll. The homely strains of Miss Ellen O'Leary appealed to a circle whose approbation was well worth possessing. Sir Gavan Duffy came prominently before a new generation as the historian of Davis and Young Ireland. Richard Dowling had written a story of Western Ire-

land whose power had suggestions not unworthy of
Hugo. In Richard Ashe King's "Wearing of the
Green," and Miss Gallaher's "Thy Name is Truth,"
the Land League afterwards found illustration in fiction.
With John Augustus O'Shea we had entered a new
Bohemia. Miss Katherine Tynan won speedy fame
with poetry which showed that a welcome new personality had strayed to Irish fields, though neither the
spirit nor the form of the work was Celtic as we had
understood it. Miss Fanny Parnell, in a few of her
lyrics, gave expression to the tumultuous life and passion
of the time. A little later, in one or two Ulster stories,
Mrs. Pender showed a touch which was rare in Irish
newspaper novels. James Murphy told stirring stories
of Wexford and Wicklow in '98. P. G. Smyth, a
western journalist, had given us in "The Wild Rose
of Lough Gill," an excellent story of 1641. Miss Mary
Killgallen, under the pseudonym of "Merva," had
published Irish verses of more than promise; Miss
Una Ashworth Taylor once in a while wrote an Irish
poem of striking merit. A young Ulsterman, Patrick
MacManus ("Slieve Donard") was the author of poems
and stories which were the signs of a new Griffin or
Banim, till his untimely death, in 1886, snapped the
hope. In those days the *Nation* Office in Dublin, was
the only literary centre which Ireland possessed; and it
was by no means unworthy of its traditions. It had
previously been the training-ground of Thomas Sexton,
Richard Dowling, John Francis O'Donnell, and others.
The thoughts of many young writers turned to it with
hope, and it really inspired much effort.

The mention of the *Nation* suggests T. D. Sullivan.

His songs that may live were written before the eighties. To our young writers and workers he was, and is, the genial-hearted grand-sire who tells pleasant stories and sings merry songs in the evening-time of life. With two or three well-known exceptions, his best lyrics have been light or lightsome. He has been a sunny-hearted minnesinger finding his way by troublous paths and stormy political windings. I doubt if any Irish singer is more popular than he by an Irish peasant's chimney-corner. Epics have died while " Deep in Canadian Woods " is as popular as ever. Mrs. Bryant in her " Celtic Ireland " describes the Gaelic bards as having their hands on the strings of the popular heart. Something similar might have been said of T.D.S. in the Land League years. The western peasant who on one occasion when he wanted to libel a neighbour, to scarify him in rhyme, wrote up to Mr. Sullivan for a " poetic licence " to do so, had not an altogether unusual notion of his powers and privileges.

The finest Irish singer of that period was at the other side of the Atlantic. John Boyle O'Reilly was a true poet. One strong impression which the spirit of his poetry leaves, is that, like the personality behind it, it is manly and loveable ; that it has its hours of real exaltation, just as the manly and loveable natures in the world have their spells of rapture, subtly stealing on them even amid the heat and the burthen. His books, " Songs of the Southern Seas," " Statues from the Block," " In Bohemia," and others, cannot be summarised easily. Here we have the sensitive lyrist, the idealist, the rebel, the eager-hearted lover of humanity, the Christian, Bohemian, socialist, the poet always.

The fine range of sympathy, the noble humanity that find voice in his poems, found illustration in his life. Of leaders of latter-day Irish thought he was the most human. No one saw more in poor humanity, or loved it better for devotion to " any good cause at all." He kept his splendid faith, his enthusiasm that could blaze or be calm as the religion of a martyr. Young Ireland found in him a type of everything that was worthy in Young Irelandism, and in his Irish songs an unfailing inspiration. He stood in the nineteenth century like a disciple who remembered the Master.

The early eighties saw the beginning of an Irish literary movement whose full result and force are being felt to-day. It did not arise in the Ireland at home, but in Southwark, a district of London whose immediate neighbourhood has memories and associations of Marlowe and Chaucer. If the Celtic intellectual awakenings of the last decade succeed in realising the hopes of those who watched every opening with anxious interest, the Irish student of after days may have kindly thoughts of certain scenes in Southwark. They will not be alien ground to him. Beginnings were made here of a kind as worthy as those of which Ferguson dreamed when he " walked through Ballinderry in the springtime." A young civil servant, born in Kinvara, Co. Galway, and author at a tender age of an Irish drama,* here began in conjunction with a few enthusiastic friends, an Irish revival which led to many such awakenings in Great Britain. Francis A. Fahy, if he were not diffident and careless of distinction, might have won fame long since.

---

* " The Last of the O'Learys."

Of his right to it the reader will have more evidence when I have finished the story of the Southwark Irish Literary Club. This body was preceded by a juvenile organisation, the Southwark Junior Irish Literary Club. It was at a time when politics held fast the souls of the vast majority of the Irish people. As far as many sections of them were concerned an effort to turn their thoughts to literature might well seem useless. Francis Fahy himself, and his young friends, were, I must admit, as ardent politicians as any. But they had far-reaching literary and educational projects as well. There were in existence when they took up their new work a couple of Junior Irish Literary Clubs, and a central council, consisting of Miss Skeffington Thompson (author of an Irish novel, " Moy O'Brien," and an " Irish Birthday Book," bearing the *nom-de-plume*, " Melusine "), Mrs. A. M. Sullivan, Mrs. Rae, and other ladies. The work in hand was a wide one. Notwithstanding the political ferment, thousands of Irish children in London were growing up Irish in nothing but in name. Now came an effort to make them Irish of the Irish, to teach them Irish history and many things kindred, to brighten their minds with national songs, stories, and traditions, to develop their now dim Celtic talents. Francis Fahy in those days was an enthusiast and a tireless worker. Very soon under his management, and that of his friends, the Southwark branch of the Junior Literary Club was far and away the most effective of all of them. In 1882, despite the growing political stress, its fame had travelled a long way beyond Southwark. Others besides children were glad to drop in to the meetings in the

Francis A. Fahy.

Surrey Rooms, Blackfriars Road. The papers prepared by Fahy, embodying notes, suggestions, subjects to be taught, lectures to be given, songs to be learned, examinations to take place, Irish prizes to be furnished, children's Irish concerts to be arranged,—have been preserved. They are suggestive of a Government department in their minuteness and complexity, and illustrate quite a system of Irish national education. Sunday was the only day available for the work, and cheerfully the young men and women gave up their Sabbath afternoons to its performance.* Lessons and lectures in Irish history, geography, and other subjects, as well as singing and essay-writing, were zealously attended to. There were monthly children's concerts, and periodical prize-distribution. Few Irish literary men of the new generation have set themselves to more necessary work. Bright features of some of the gatherings were songs written and sung by Fahy, whose muse had awoken, her earliest notes possessing much of the lyric sweetness that charmed a much wider audience somewhat later. A Child's Irish Song Book which he edited was referred to by Sir John Pope Hennessy in an article in the *Nineteenth Century* called " What the Irish read." Fahy went further, and wrote a Child's Irish History in Rhyme, which was highly lauded by the press of the period, as an effort as happy as it was simple. It was admirably suited to its tender audience.

Needless to say, some of the proceedings at the youthful meetings had their humorous touches. On one

* Amongst the teachers were F. A. Fahy, J. T. Kelly, D. J. Sweeney, W. Fahy, Miss Hicks, Miss Quinn, Miss Fahy and Miss Lanigan.

occasion after a lecturer had reviewed some English charges against Irishmen, and taken special pains to show either their falsity, or circumstances which explained them, turned to a healthy, sturdy boy, and in order to test how far he had grasped the lecture, asked : " Now if an English boy were to say to you that the Irish are a lazy, drunken, thriftless race, how would you answer him ? " " I'd knock him down, sir," was the prompt rejoinder. Some of the juvenile essays on Irish subjects were not less entertaining. " When an Irishman drinks," wrote one small boy, " he is very excitable. Whiskey is the favourite drink, and soon gets into the head. An Englishman could drink twice as much and it would not have the same effect upon him. It is often said that Irishmen fight for fun. When they fight like this they are called savages. But if the English make quarrels with other nations and get the Irish to win their battles, they are called heroes, as in the case of Tel-el-Kebir."

A new move was made in January, 1883. Rich success had crowned the labours of those who had undertaken the national education of the Irish children of South London, but the adult element around them needed quite as much ministering care. They themselves were keenly conscious of the want of a congenial Irish centre, as intellectual as they could make it, and though in the heart of London, yet racy of the home soil. Enthusiasm led to action, and the Southwark Irish Literary Club came into existence, the teachers in the Junior Club being amongst the first band of pioneers. Till September 1885, the meetings were held (as a rule once a week) in the Surrey Rooms, after that date in the Bath Street

Hall, London Road. The Club's appropriate motto was *Sgar an solus*—"Spread the Light." Its objects were the cultivation of Irish history, art, and literature, and the providing of a medium of social and intellectual intercourse for Irish people of both sexes. Amongst the means to attain these objects were lectures, original essays, national concerts and dramatic performances, contributions to the press, the publication and sale of cheap Irish literature, the formation of a Lecture League, for the purpose of supplying lectures on Irish subjects to associations requiring them, and lastly a lending library. This Southwark Library has a history, and the following of its fortunes brings us over some main lines of the literary movement of the past ten years. It has had its woes, trials, vicissitudes; there were days when in truth it looked "poor, and old, and very sad," as Mangan sings; it weathered many storms, and now and then seemed much the worse for them; it wearied the souls of many sturdy librarians, and in turn seemed weary of life itself. But it lived, and grew, and brightened; and now, after many days, looking stately and prosperous, in all the glory and glow of glass cases and gleaming firelight, it meets your gaze in the Irish Literary Society, London (like the rejuvenated spirit of Irish Literature, I hear from some one facetious and fanciful). It has been the literary Lia Fail of the little Southwark band. If there were a "continuity" question in our literary movement, there is its visible sign —— But I must return to plain history.

The Southwark programme was a most ambitious one, all the circumstances considered. Though the active workers were never a large number, it was carried

out with unfailing spirit through many years of political
tension, scanty finances, and trying circumstances of
other kinds.   At the preliminary meeting held on
January 4th, 1883, a number of ladies and gentlemen
present formed themselves into a preliminary committee.
In July a new committee was formed.   F. A. Fahy was
president, John T. Kelly, secretary.   The work that
year consisted largely of concerts, readings, and the like.
A wise beginning was made in giving those who rallied
to the Club a thorough insight into Irish popular literature.   An "Irish National Reciter" was compiled, and
other work mapped out.   A few lectures were given,
including one by Mr. T. D. Sullivan, on "The National
Songs of Ireland," and others by members on Irish
imaginative, historical, and geological subjects.   At
one meeting a member urged the desirability of holding
an Irish Eisteddfod.   The lectures were a god-send to the
Irish of London who had aspirations which the newspapers could not satisfy.   Another year saw the new
association on a much firmer basis.   Great progress was
made in some directions.   The contributions to the Irish
press of a few members had attracted considerable
attention, notably the lyrics of Francis Fahy, over
the *nom-de-plume* of "Dreolin," as well as a few
swinging ditties by J. T. K.   The reports in the
Dublin papers of the Club's proceedings had set young
Irishmen at home a-thrill with the desire for Irish
studies, researches, and writings of a character similar
to those of their brethren in Southwark.   We have
advanced so far in the decade since then that it is difficult to realise how novel and appealing was this work
to a rising generation.   The lectures alone in this year

c

would have furnished a creditable record.   Towards the
autumn the Club had become so widely known that
Irishmen who had achieved distinction in various walks
were glad to be found on its platform.   Mr. Barry
O'Brien, known as the author of Irish historical works,
lectured to it in November on " Political Evolution in
Ireland." The Rev. Percy Miles, M.A., of Trinity
came later to treat " Irish National Poetry " in a style
rather unfamiliar in Trinity.   Writing to John T. Kelly
from the *Nation* office on Christmas Eve, accepting the
presidency of the Society for the next year, Mr. T. D.
Sullivan said :

"The Southwark Literary Club is rapidly winning
distinction in the field of Irish literature.   I have often
wondered how it has happened that in one small section
of London such a number of clever and gifted young
Irishmen have been got together.   The Club is well
represented in the little volume entitled ' Emerald
Gems ' just issued from this office, a collection, I do not
hesitate to say, which is worthy to take a place by the
side of the ' Spirit of the Nation.'   I am very proud of
the volume, as somehow I regard those young poets of
the *Nation, Weekly News* and *Young Ireland*, as ' My own
boys ' "

John T. Kelly was one of the men who made the Southwark Club, as well as the Dublin National Literary
Society of the present day, and as we shall meet him
frequently, a word regarding him will be in season here.
Born in '64 in Clonmacnoise, he was educated at Blackrock College, and came to London in 1882.   He wrote
stirring and stormful lyrics for the Dublin papers, and
occasionally in his amatory ditties, which came at will,

JOHN T. KELLY.

he was not unlike one of the characters referred to by Gerald Griffin,

> " Who sigh like Boreas, and make love like war."

He seemed born to storm barricades, or lead forlorn hopes. " Send us war in our time, O Lord," must have been a frequent prayer of his. He had been a close student of Irish and continental literature, but I have no doubt that he considered Casey's " Rising of the Moon," and Koerner's " Song of the Sword," as worth some dozen dramas. In one of Fahy's " Club Poems," entitled " Three Old Men," he is represented as thus voicing his sentiments and recollections :—

> " For many a year as Hon'rary Sec.
> I held that Club in my open palm,
> And steered it as near as I could to wreck,
> And veered it as far as I could from calm.

> " For I loved most the whiff of the battle smoke,
> The clangour of conflict, the onset's din,
> My spirit leaped out when the war-cry woke,
> I rushed to the vanguard thro' thick and thin.

> " I was never so glad as when most abused,
> I was never at peace save in open war,
> I never knew comfort save when ill-used,
> I smelt the field of the fight afar.

> " With the sword of defiance I cleaved in twain,
> The doubter's doubting, the coward's dread,
> As in days of yore on the ' tented ' plain,
> I struck wherever I saw a head."

In the club days this side of his character often appeared uppermost. Beneath it was a very manly nature and sympathies much deeper than the casual observer believed. He was a good lecturer, a stirring speaker, but a better organiser. He was, in fact, the strong hand of the Southwark Club. He was often

marked contrast to his constant friend, "Dreolin."
Fahy had inexhaustible humour and ready wit; but it
did not need an acute critic to notice that the sallies
were sometimes mere devices to hide the pathos
of his nature. His acquirements and gifts were as
diverse as his character. He had mastered in a short
time several modern languages and authors, had coursed
through the Irish language and its literature, written the
raciest Irish songs of our time, turned off squibs and
sketches welcome to the laughter-loving, had worked
heart and soul for the Club, planned many projects
beyond it, and delivered thoughtful Irish lectures in
every quarter of London. He wrote poems with happy
fancies and melody, and lyrics with living pictures of
the Irish hearth and the people's ways. Others of the
young men were beginning to find their Irish talents, as
we shall find in due course.

Special features of this year were "Gaelic Nights,"
when all the contributions, songs, stories, and sketches
were in Gaelic—mostly Irish Gaelic, but occasionally in
the Scotch and Welsh dialects. A lecture was given on
one occasion on Ireland's national literature by Mr.
T. J. Flannery of the Gaelic Union, who is well-known
as an Irish scholar, and as a contributor to the *Nation*,
Irishman, Gaelic Journal, etc. Amongst the matters read
on those "Gaelic Nights" were newly published contributions from one who was afterwards to win the
highest honours in the field—Dr. Douglas Hyde. The
club also published a little book of Gaelic poems which
like all its productions and compilations had a large
and rapid sale.

The great feature of this year's programme, and one

for which the Club became widely noted, was its
" Original Nights." Good Irish work in poem, story,
sketch, and ballad, was specially prepared for such
" nights "—including most of the pieces which " Dreolin "
and others afterwards contributed to the press. The
series was opened by Fahy in a humorous poem called
" Our Original Night," which told the jealousy of present leaders and great spirits of the past, because of
the transcendent lore which would be offered at these
gatherings. The wrathful ghosts of Irish geniuses were
round his bed the previous night—he tried to mollify
them—asked them to the Club, but

> " ' Never,' they cried with much cursing and muttering,
> ' Faded the laurels we thought ever green,
> Henceforth our works will but wrap Long-Lane butterine,*
> Or only on second-hand bookstalls be seen.
> " Little we'd mind—'twould have moved our hilarity—
> Had you stopped short at those lectures not bright,
> But you struck a foul blow at our famed popularity
> When you laid out this Original Night.' "

The subjects chosen were delightfully diverse. Martial
Irish ballads were followed by racy sketches of Irish
country life. Contributions of the latter character were
plentiful. They brought happy touches and glimpses of
the home-world around those Celtic wanderers. In fact
not only was the Club keeping warm a Gaelic spirit,
and inspiring to literary effort, but it was a rendezvous,
a little theatre of congenial spirits, common ties, and
common interests ; not the less interesting for the
knowledge of little romances in the background.   •

The year 1885 was one of remarkable progress ;
and young Irishmen of literary leanings and popular

---

* One of the members kept a butter-shop in Long Lane, Bermondsey.

J. A. O'SHEA.

sympathies looked to Southwark as a centre of hope.
The guides of the association were in fact *Nation* young
men of a new generation, without, however, an organ to
popularise their views. In this year Mr. John Augustus
O'Shea found his way to the Club, and was one of its
most faithful friends ever after. The enthusiasm, Irish
ideals, and animal spirits of the young workers appealed
at once to the Irish Bohemian. There was now a long
array of contributors at hand in the persons of F. A.
Fahy, J. T. Kelly, John A. O'Connell (who wrote
excellent Irish poems), P. J. Keawell (an active worker
in those years, who contributed personal recollections of
Charles Kickham, and country sketches), T. McSweeney
(Irish scholar and humorist), Thomas Glynn (a genial
Connaught man, stored with the homely lore of the
people, and whose subject might be anything from the
Liberator to the latest street-ballads), Peter O'Leary
(a son of the people, belonging to an earlier genera-
tion, and deep in ideas upon ancient Ireland), J. G.
Meagher (author of good poems and thoughtful lectures),
Robert May (an authority on the Irish drama), John
Cronin (who inclined to Irish philosophic studies), M. J.
Finnerty (humorist), John Lynch (a kindly Kerryman,
with a touch of Goldsmith's nature and Goldsmith's
style), Mrs. Haffenden (contributor of foreign sketches
and anecdotes), William Fahy and D. J. Sweeney,
whose *rôle* was public speaking. J. M. Reynolds, H. P.
O'Reilly, and many other workers came a little later.
Amongst the lecturers this year were John Augustus
O'Shea, who discoursed on " Irish Land-marks in
London," and John Redmond, M.P., whose subject
was " Wexford in '98." The mere titles of the other

lectures show the worthy fields into which those students carried their researches. Here are some of them : " Pat in Foreign Parts," " Clarence Mangan," " Gerald Griffin," " Irish songs of Wit and Humour," " Kickham," " Ancient Irish Civilization," " O'Connell," " Folk-lore," " Irish Dramatists," and " The Geraldines."

In the course of the year there was a strong desire on the part of the Committee to publish a selèction of the poems of Charles Kickham, but unfortunately, like various kindred wishes, it was not carried out. Had our young friends been better supported, especially financially, there is no doubt whatever that Irish literature for the people would have received memorable additions in the eighties. '86 was in some respects a year of trial for the Southwark association, but its literary work withal went on with renewed vigour. The " Original Nights " were more original than ever ; and several new supporters had gravitated towards the Club. I find an entry in a member's note-book of the year, which introduces initials that were soon to become well known to Irish *littérateurs.* " 1886, January 17th ; First appearance at the Club of the renowned D. J. O'D. and brother. So awe-stricken at the learned looks of the members, that they did not dare to venture inside." Mr. O'Donoghue, though at first so retiring, was soon a force in Southwark. While Fahy, Kelly and their friends trod poetic or imaginative highways, the future friend of forgotten bards gave papers and lectures upon every imaginable illustration of Irish achievement. Once he lectured upon " France and Ireland," bringing an array of facts to prove that France had treated Ireland

shabbily notwithstanding the latter's long list of services, and that the writers of no other nation in Europe
betrayed such ignorance of Irish circumstances as hers.
The lecture was duly reported, and soon came a
challenge to mortal combat from an indignant French-
man. The Club interfered, no blood was spilled, and
O'D. went on with his usual work. His brother, Mr.
Griffin O'Donoghue, was hardly less active. Early in
the year the Irish press and public saluted a racy
and musical volume of " Irish Songs and Poems," by
" Dreolin." Most of them had been specially written
for the " Original Nights," and for many reasons the
publication and the immediate favourable reception were
matters of direct personal interest to the members.
There were some capital lectures that year, Mr. O'Shea,
Mr. Fitzgerald Molloy, and Dr. Rentoul, now an Ulster
M.P., bearing off most of the principal honours. One
autumn eve in 1887 (September 21st), Mr. Justin
McCarthy, M.P. lectured on " The Literature of '48."
The occasion had another interest, in the fact that Sir
Charles Gavan Duffy was in the chair. To most of the
audience it almost seemed as if the dead had arisen to
study the present. For Sir Charles was essentially a
figure of a dead generation. The Irish Phœnix had
arisen many times from its ashes since, on his turning in
despair from Ireland, he had used the most imaginative
phrase of his life, telling of a national corpse on the
dissecting table. To the young students his later life
was all but unknown—he was to them the colleague of
Thomas Davis, who had worked for ideals like their own
in buoyant days before the Great Famine had buried a
whole Irish world of hope, pride, and pleasantry ; or

D. J. O'Donoghue.

before the remnants of a broken race went down to the
sea in coffin-ships. He had stepped into a little world
that would have charmed Thomas Davis — though,
curiously enough, amongst those who were there to
greet him was the representative of a movement with
which Young Ireland could have had no sympathy ;—the
very head centre of æstheticism himself—more curious
still, that this same representative should be the son of
" Speranza." Sir Charles told the young men something about the magic of Young Irelandism, as he had
known it : and passed out again from that vivid little
Ireland in London.   He was destined to come in touch
with its leading workers in a later day when many
helpers had rallied to their side, when their schemes
were broader, and when Irish intellectual movements
had reached brighter stages.   Another instance of the
growing intellectual gravitation towards Southwark
occurred this year, when Mr. Edmund Downey (F.
M. Allen) appeared on the scene to read some Irish
humorous sketches from that volume which began his
run of real literary luck—" Through Green Glasses." It
had just been published, receiving an almost embarassing
amount of critical benediction, Mr. Gladstone leading off
the chorus.   Mr. Downey was too modest and retiring
to take a prominent part in the work at Southwark, but
thenceforward he was the fast friend of the young men
and their projects, and could always be reckoned upon
as an enthusiast who would serve in a quiet way.   In
succeeding years, in the midst of a busy literary career,
he was always ready to give a helping hand to Irish
work of a national or literary character, no matter how
local it might be.

The influence of the club continued to widen in
1888–9. Some who came to lecture remained to be
constant workers. Fahy, Kelly, D. J. O'Donoghue, D.
P. Moran, J. G. O'Keeffe, and the present writer had
frequent occasion to take the platform, but in the two
years under consideration many willing helpers came to
the front. One night it was Mr. Daniel Crilly, M.P.,
who lectured on Fanny Parnell. By thè way, on the
occasion of Mr. Crilly's lecture (it was in March, 1888),
a young man found his way to the Club, who was just
beginning a highly remarkable Irish literary career, and
who found in the Club's proceedings an attraction
which brought him over miles of London many a time
afterwards, till gradually he became one of ourselves.
We had met his name in the *Irish Fireside* and in the
Dublin University Review (edited by T. W. Rolleston,
whose acquaintance was to come somewhat later). In
appearance he was tall, slight, and mystic of the
mystical. His face was not so much dreamy as
haunting : a little weird even—so that really if one
were to meet him on an Irish mountain in the moonlight
he would assuredly hasten away to the nearest fireside
with a story of a new and genial ghost which had
crossed his path. He spoke in a hushed, musical, eerie
tone : a tone which had constant suggestions of the
faery world, of somebody " in 'em " (that is, in the
councils of the fairies), as we say in Ireland. His
name was W. B. Yeats. He lectured for us shortly
afterwards, bringing with him on that occasion a gifted
Irishman, who also was destined to be a comrade later
on—Dr. John Todhunter. Some of us thought till then
that we had a very tolerable acquaintance with the

ways and doings of the Irish fairies, but Yeats' lecture
(of course it was on the good people) was something of
a revelation to us—in fact he spoke as one who took his
information firsthand. His only error was to speak
unduly of the *soulths* and *sheogues* of his own county,
but the South had a sturdy champion in John Augustus
O'Shea, who gave it as his experience that there were
more fairies on a square foot of Knockshegowna than in
all the County Sligo.   To Yeats' next lecture came
Miss Katherine Tynan, who was on a visit to the
English capital. Mr. J. F. Hogan, who was not then
M.P. for Mid-Tipperary, and had not given up his soul
to "Imperial" schemes that are 'least popular in the
constituency he represents, was also one of our '88
lecturers : a right pleasant one, too.   Mr. Halliday
Sparling, most genial of socialists, discoursed to us on
Irish Minstrelsy, and the literature of '98, and when he
thought that a brilliant circle of lecturers had necessarily
exhausted every conceivable home subject, he turned
our attention to Ireland's influence upon Iceland and
her literature.   Mrs. Sophie Bryant, D.Sc., authoress of
" Celtic Ireland," interested us with an eloquent and
clear-sighted lecture on " The Early Races of Ireland."
Early in '89, Eugene Davis was chairman at one
meeting, and had an interesting word to say upon the
subject of Irish poetry. He was then serving on the
staff of the *Nation*, a paper to which many of us were
contributors, and to which we were attached for its
traditions and its present work on behalf of Irish
literary developments. One of the '88 lectures I have
not spoken of till now, as in connection with it I have
to tell of an idea whose working extended through the

next two years. Mr. Michael MacDonagh, who was rapidly coming to the front as a journalist (he had succeeded T. P. O'Connor as the *Freeman* sketch-writer in the House of Commons) and as a writer of Irish essays, was brought to our midst by an energetic secretary. Mr. MacDonagh had been writing a series of articles on Irish graves in England, and it had been an old dream of Mr. Kelly's to see something done for a few of the graves which had been most undeservedly neglected. He thereupon wrote to Mr. MacDonagh, requesting that the grave of John Francis O'Donnell should not be forgotten. The reply was to the effect that it was O'Donnell's neglected grave in Kensal Green which had suggested the series. Eventually Mr. Mac-Donagh lectured at the Club on the subject of these Irish graves, and on the night of the lecture a committee was formed with the two-fold object of publishing O'Donnell's poems, and putting his grave in a decent condition. The handsome volume of " Poems of John Francis O'Donnell " issued at Christmas, 1890, stands unquestionably as one of the most creditable additions made to Irish literature in the latter half of our century. It was a worthy work to bring it forth from the living death of old newspaper files ; but unfortunately O'Donnell's is only one rescued reputation amongst many lost—one life from the pitiful death and oblivion that have dogged Irish writers who wrote in other days for their own people. However, we may rejoice that even one bright reputation has been saved. The book is O'Donnell's monument, and Mr. Kelly may be proud to be the sculptor. He was an enthusiastic editor ; and in Mr. Richard Dowling who wrote an

introduction to the volume (thus another Irish writer
linked to Southwark) he found one who understood and
cordially appreciated his enthusiasm. I should mention
that in an appeal for aid in the matter, written at the
outset by Mr. John Augustus O'Shea, there was the
best and most correctly critical eulogy of O'Donnell's
poetry which I have seen from any pen.

In the light of subsequent events, and indeed for
its own sake, the following letter, received by the editor
soon after the O'Donnell publication had been issued, will
be read with interest:

" VILLA MARGUERITE, NICE,
"*Feb.* 23*rd* [1891.]

" Dear Sir,—
        " I thank you for O'Donnell's poems,
which are produced in a very creditable manner, and
will be his best monument. His wife lives in France,
and feels a warm sympathy with all you have been
doing for his memory.

" What you say of the need for publishing the verse
and prose of men and women who have helped the
national cause for the last generation or two is very
true, and has often been the subject of my thoughts.
The poems of ' Mary of Cork,' the late Judge O'Hagan,
and Charles Kickham, are cases in point.

" I have often thought of forming a small Limited
Liability Company for this purpose. The Irish race in
Ireland, England, and America ought to buy a large
number of little books published at the size and price of
Cassell's National Library. I dare say I could get the
capital for the purpose, but it would need the enthusiasm

of young men to work it. Their enthusiasm is a more important element than money, and I would not be a party to putting any pecuniary obligation on them.

" If you and the friends you speak of think well of this idea, I will send you some preliminary inquiries to make. I am going to Rome early next month, and will be absent for a month or five weeks, but after I return I would have leisure for the question.

" Very faithfully yours,

" C. GAVAN DUFFY."

" Of course the books I name are only a specimen of what ought and might be produced."

A few words only are necessary to describe the position of affairs at this time. After 1889 the scene changes from Southwark. In 1890 we decided to remove to the neighbouring district of Clapham. Most of the members were residing there—some good workers had gone to Dublin—and Southwark was not as convenient as in earlier years. The transplanted Society did not do quite as well as before, though the little band of active workers had more literary schemes in progress than ever. Early in 1891 we decided at a meeting in the Clapham Reform Club to change the name of the association to the Irish Literary Society, London, a mere local title seeming inadvisable. The library of the Southwark Club passed with us in our change of name, and in some ways things went on as before. Our ranks had, however, been thinned, but the efforts of the

constant workers grew more ambitious. The *Nation* of
the early months of 1891 contains occasional particulars
of our progress and purposes. We had decided to
abandon public lectures for some time, to devote our
energies to solid literary work, to meet frequently at one
another's houses and discuss our projects. Amongst
the ideas of the Society were the publication of works of
neglected Irish authors, the collection of Irish literary
material, contributions on Irish subjects to current
literature, and most important of all, the establishment
of a library of original Irish books. We believed that
by quiet and steady work, by the earnest exertion of
whatever powers we possessed, we could do something
towards the extension and popularisation of Irish
literature. The provisional committee consisted of F.
A. Fahy, D. J. O'Donoghue, W. P. Ryan, Thomas
Boyd, J. G. O'Keeffe, with John T. Kelly as secretary.
We started a monthly manuscript magazine, to which
all the members were invited to contribute. In 1891,
with the seething agitation consequent on the Parnell
question all around, it was not the easiest matter in the
world to conduct an Irish Literary Society. We heard
the crashing of tumultuous waves even in our quiet little
haven of literature. But we worked steadily on, coming
no closer to politics at our re-unions than to make jovial
remarks over the fierce opposition of the newspapers to
which some of us were attached. The *Nation* was our
good friend for a time. Under the editorial charge of
an able young Catholic University man, Robert
Donovan, it was thought that there was still a future
before it. Mr. Donovan did really good work, his
knowledge and his ideals were of the right kind, his

Irish literary sympathies excellent. He left the dying *Nation*, however, for the *National Press*, subsequently joining the *Freeman's Journal*, settling down, I fear, like many another journalist to be a lost child of literature. The *Nation* died soon after, or rather it was incorporated with the *Irish Catholic*. The Irish Literary Society, London, lost a friend, on Mr. Donovan's withdrawal. A thorough one went in the person of John T. Kelly, who like other Southwarkians, sought " Liffey's tide and Dublin's town," for mingled patriotic and business reasons. Thus we stood when the time came for the consideration of Sir Gavan Duffy's ideas. To a large extent they harmonised with our own ; we were perfectly willing to work as Sir Charles suggested, and we saw some measure of poetic justice in having one of Davis's colleagues, and the founder of the original Irish Library, at the head of a new scheme, and a new library fifty years after. It was decided to draw up a list of the books which we considered should be published, the material we had at hand, our plans and resources, and the means we thought advisable for the better distribution and popularisation of the new volumes. I need only say that our literary plan of campaign was a wide and well-considered one. Sir Charles did not, however, move as fast as we did, and towards the end of 1891 we saw little prospect of a new Irish Library, unless it could be started upon our own independent lines.

In December came a new development. For some time an idea had been growing in the minds of some members that it was useless to work locally, however well. Some of us had thought from the outset, also,

as the *Nation* references will show, that unless we devoted
ourselves to original work rather than mere re-publica-
tion, and organised a wide and thorough popular
programme, our intellectual usefulness to Ireland would
be next to an unknown quantity. Mr. W. B. Yeats, who
was as much drawn to the Southwark circle as if it were
a novel race of *sheogues*, discussed various questions
connected with the Irish Literary Society with Mr. D.
J. O'Donoghue in the congenial shadow of the British
Museum.   Mr. Yeats was decidedly of opinion, too, that
the work might be attempted upon a more ambitious
scale. He offered to induce Mr. T. W. Rolleston and
others to throw themselves into the Irish literary movement, and to summon a meeting of sympathisers and
willing workers for an early date. The proposal was
cordially approved of, and the meeting awaited with
interest. It came off at Mr. Yeats' house in Chiswick
on the 28th of December, 1891. This brings me to a
memorable development whose history will be found in
a subsequent chapter.

I have written in vain if the sympathetic Irish reader
should close this chapter without feeling a *grah* for
Southwark. It is surely not difficult to see the work
that was done, the seed sown, the spirit fostered, the
workers trained in that Surrey hall, through the stormful
years of a national struggle. The sweeter background
of kindly associations and clinging friendships, of bright
enthusiasm, delightful social gatherings, and mayhap
occasional romances, it is scarcely my province to touch
upon, links of gold though they be in the chain of
life in London. The little haunt would by no means
tempt the average tourist. John Augustus O'Shea

was fond of calling it "a cut-throat street." Even so—not mansions and Arcadian haunts alone are sacred either to the spirit of literature or the spirit of memory.

III.

T is time to consider the intellectual developments of a Celtic character which were
visible in Irish centres at home during this
Eighty decade.   After all, without Irish
literary awakenings in Ireland, without movements
corresponding to those in London or elsewhere, is not
the dream of an Irish revival a sorry and a useless
one? Ireland is of course the inspiration of all the outer
movements ; the thoughts of their workers turn to her,
bright to their fancies as she is, lovely within her " four
bright seas."   But not only should she be the centre
and source of inspiration, she should also lead the way.
It is owing to accidental and temporary circumstances
that any Irish intellectual movement originates in London or any other foreign centre. Beginning there, it
is meant that it should end in Ireland, be moulded
throughout by Irish ideals and aims, and be influenced
in no degree whatever by the Teutonic influences about
it.   Every Irish literature must have its roots deep in
the racy home soil : a literature peculiar solely and

simply to an Ireland abroad is as undesirable, and almost as impossible, as a literature peculiar to the cross-channel mariners.

A movement of great promise was initiated in Dublin in March, 1888. One of the prime movers was Gerald C. Pelly, a medical student from the West. Sir Charles Duffy in his *Nation* days had exhorted young Irish writers to study the history of their country in order that their works might " treasure her legends, eternalize her traditions, and people her scenery." These words had impressed Mr. Pelly, and eventually he determined to form an association of Irish writers whose guiding aim would be the realisation of this duty. He discussed the idea with two friends, Augustine F. Downey, and the late M. D. Wyer, B.L., who had derived their inspiration from far different sources. A society that would carry out their wishes was projected. At first the title of " The Irish National Literary Society " was considered a suitable one, but was not pressed on account of the political significance attached to the word " national." Finally Wyer and Downey adopted the name " Pan-Celtic," as appropriate and comprehensive enough. The new society was to be essentially non-political, non-sectarian, and entirely a working organisation. The membership was restricted to those who had previously published a story, essay, sketch, or poem in any Irish magazine or newspaper of standing, or who possessed a literary knowledge of the Celtic language. It was on these lines that the Pan-Celtic Society commenced its career on the 1st of March, 1888.

Pelly was then nearly twenty-three years of age, and

an active worker. Like Downey and John T. Kelly,
he had spent some years at Blackrock College. His
first poetical compositions appeared in the *Western News*,
but he was afterwards well-known as a contributor of
prose and verse to the Dublin papers. Over the *noms-
de-plume* of " Gerald " and " G. Cieppe," he wrote
novels, tales, and sketches descriptive of Connaught life
and traditions. The more homely the subject the more
successful his treatment of it. Over and over again he
emphasized the fact that young Irish writers would find
their finest literary fields in their own parishes. He
made many excursions into the wide treasure-worlds of
Gaelic song and story, and did much in the Pan-Celtic
days to bring home the knowledge of their riches to
others. Downey was much the same age as his friend,
and at that time, too, a medical student. He had previously conducted a literary society called " The Dalton
Williams Students' Association," and was full of Irish
projects. He was an admirable type of the young
Irishman of a new generation that had cast away
doubt, morbid thought, and irresolution, that faced
the future with ardour. Suave and cultured, he
was yet essentially a revolutionary. He possessed
much literary power, was a graceful and persuasive
speaker, an enthusiast to the finger-tips, a Celt of the
Celts. Tall, handsome, and dressed with scrupulous
care, you would think on your first glimpse of him that
he was what Robert Buchanan has described as a
" superfine young man." The mistake would be speedily
patent to you. He had thought out his own conclusions
on many pressing Irish problems. You would find him
as thorough in his own way as Oliver Cromwell. His

opinions on Irish education were very candid. Until Irishmen were educated as Irishmen the country would continue its downward rush. We should learn that neither nationality, literature, nor Irish industries would be benefitted by " educating " the young men not only to ignore, but despise Ireland and everything Irish. Till we put a stop to the cram system of English " whiggification," misnamed " National Education," till we insisted upon the educational systems of the country being based upon the rational principle of Celtism—all our efforts would be in vain. Davis, he pointed out, knew this, and so did Mitchel. As to compulsory education, he considered it was no *remedy* until we had first changed the *rationale* of treatment. How was this to be done ? He would answer—theoretically, by teaching Irish history (as well as English or Greek history) in every school and college, by making it not optional, but compulsory ; by offering every inducement to boys and girls to learn Gaelic ; and, furthermore, we should carry on a continual fight until we had succeeded in replacing the matter required by the Intermediate curricula by works written by Irish authors. Pope should give way to Mangan, Macaulay to Davis, and so on. This, naturally enough, would encourage Irish authors to write and Irish publishers to publish. The Intermediate System was simply a continuation of the National Board System, and was an agency for the sale of books published in England. Thus, Dublin publishers were only agents for the sale of English-printed books. An important industry was decaying : compositors, book-binders, etc., were no longer required. We could, he added, trace the decay of the mind of Ireland to the garbage on which it was fed. In fine, " Celtism " was the only hope, the only safe-guard. We should go in for intellectual as well as political Home Rule. Sturdy opinions of this nature were advocated by Dr. Downey at every opportunity. Under the *nom-de-plume* of " Diarmiud O'Duibhne " (a Gaelic hero) he contributed poems, some of them of strong native fibre, to the Dublin and provincial journals.

Matthew Daly Wyer was one of the men whose convictions were driven home and deepened in the fever years of the Land League. He was the son of an evicted tenant, and earned plank-bed honours during Mr. Forster's *régime*. For some years he was a professor at Blackrock and Clongowes Wood Colleges, and was afterwards called to the bar. His literary work consisted mostly of political poems for the national papers, and leaders for the *Freeman's Journal*. The Pan-Celtic Society had no more devoted labourer while he lived.

Amongst the earliest to join were P. J. Keawell (once of Southwark), who subsequently became its treasurer ; R. J. O'Mulrenin, of Trinity College, then co-editor with Mr. John Fleming, of the *Gaelic Journal ;* Miss Teresa C. Boylan, a young Kildare poetess, who was in those years one of the brightest contributors to the Dublin papers ; and P. J. McCall. The latter was an important acquisition. Then in his twenty-seventh year he represented, perhaps, the raciest element in the association. He was a Catholic University man, possessing an intimate knowledge of Old Dublin and all its quaintness, with a knowledge nearly as thorough of the popular traits and traditions of Wexford and Wicklow. His command over metres and versification was almost as

P. J. McCALL.

peculiar as that of Clarence Mangan. His mind was stored with the drollest old songs of the people, with their idioms, superstitions and fancies. He wrote popular lyrics of a character which no Irish singer of our time has excelled ; while it is no exaggeration to say that his sketches called " Fenian Nights' Entertainments," contributed in after years to the *Shamrock*, are amongst the happiest illustrations afforded in our day of how the Irish peasant at his best can tell a story. He lives in a house in Old Dublin that teems with strange memories, and there has every-day opportunities of studying Celts both quaint and queer. No phase, flash, idiosyncrasy, or idiom escapes his observant Celtic nature.

Mr. O'Mulrenin took charge of the Gaelic department of the Pan-Celtic Society, and it was through his influence that Irish titles, such as *Ceann* for Chairman, *Rúnaire* for Secretary, were adopted by the officials.

The membership speedily increased, rooms were rented in Marlborough-street, and meetings arranged once a week. On these occasions letters and contributions from absent or country members were first read and discussed. Then came the secretary's report for the week, in which he embodied anything which might interest or affect the work of the Society. Next a paper on some Irish subject was given by a member, or some original poems rendered, after which the sense of the meeting was taken as to the advisability of forwarding them to an Irish periodical for publication. Debates were always avoided, the Society hoping for nothing from mere oratory.

In a few months the services of a band of well-

known Irish writers or workers had been secured
for the association. Amongst them were Dr. Douglas
Hyde, Dr. Todhunter, Dr. Sigerson, Miss Rose
Kavanagh, John O'Leary, Miss Ellen O'Leary,
Alfred Perceval Graves, John O'Hart, and Eugene
Davis. No one was more zealous in the cause
than Rose Kavanagh. With a weak frame, a pale
and beautiful face, whose light was alas! to be quen-
ched by an untimely death, a simple and joyous
nature, she embodied to her associates some of the
tenderest and worthiest traits of Irish womanhood.
She was then conducting a children's department in
the *Weekly Freeman* (many Irish boys and girls have
happy memories of " Uncle Remus "), and Dr. Pelly
and others recall occasion after occasion, when they saw
her in the *Freeman* office, pale and fragile, but working
out with enthusiasm some project for the development
of Irish art and literature. In these days she had many
a wish for the " glens of green Tyrone," whose sights
and traditions were so dear to her :

> " O my native mountain heather,
> How I yearned for your scent
> Through the golden summer weather,
> In the dusky city pent—
> With my heart for ever turning
> From the Liffey's noisy shore
> To the breezy braes of Ulster,
> With the heather blooming o'er!
> Every north wind was a summons,
> Very swift and very sweet,
> From the royal heath-crowned headlands,
> Seas of green corn at their feet."

Tributes to her worth and the loveableness of her
character have come to us from every quarter. Such a
nature has seldom moved so sweetly through, and passed

under such pathetic circumstances from the troubled ways of Irish life. Jacobite bards would have called her Rosaleen ; Shakespeare would have set her side by side with Imogen.

Amongst other writers, Alfred Perceval Graves, though living in England (" Irish Graves in England," as a Southwarkian styled him) was a real working member, and sent a contribution, not always of the " Father O'Flynn " type, to nearly every meeting. Mr. Louis Ely O'Carroll, B.L., was an indefatigable organiser as well as a frequent literary contributor. In Nassau Street, to which he led the Society, some of the most interesting stages of its course were run.

The organisation was now well established, and its work could be met with in the Irish papers that devoted departments to literature. The younger members were almost continually in evidence. Downey, Pelly, McCall, Miss Boylan and others were all known to readers of the popular journals. New friends kept coming in. Joseph Glynn, of Mullingar, was stored with information on most points connected with Irish biographical lore or periodical literature. He possessed the critical faculty also as well as a good literary style. James Murphy, of Maryborough, was no stranger in the Press over his Irish name (Murphy is after all not Irish) of Sheamus O'Murchadha. William S. Burke had done much work for the *Dublin Journal*, and now turned out scenic sketches, humorous stories and verses, with a ready Irish facility.* T. S. Cleary, a genial editor,

---

* For full notice of Mr. Burke's work see the account of the Bradford Irish Literary Society.

had published " Twitterings at Twilight," and was
writing verses and songs of the Land War. Daniel
Crilly, M.P., and Eugene Davis (then on the *Nation*)
became members. Robert Donovan and Frank
MacDonagh * were capable recruits from the same
office. P. O'C. MacLaughlin had long been a contributor to Irish journalism of poems and rollicking and
satiric stories. He was an invalid, and much of his
best work was done under circumstances of extreme
torture. He typifies Irish literary tragedy ; and yet the
Irish readers who know him merely know him as a
humorist! Amongst the lady members Miss Ellen
O'Leary, Miss Mary Fitzpatrick, Miss Dora Sigerson,
Miss Hester Sigerson (just coming into notice as
poetesses), Mrs. Sigerson (authoress of an Irish novel,
" A Ruined Race"), Miss M. E. Kennedy (who turned
Gaelic legends into modern verse), Miss K. B. Lawrence
(who gave papers and critiques), Mrs. Jobling (who
contributed essays), and Miss Mary Furlong (writer of
poems simple and sincere)—were pioneers from whom
much was expected and indeed received. Gradually
another bard of helpers came to the fore.

The officials were never left in need of suggestions for
the greater progress of the organisation. Many were of
opinion that it should launch an Irish Publishing Company ; others were in favour of a weekly or a fortnightly
magazine ; some thought an Irish annual would meet
the present needs. Capital, however, was needed for
these projects in greater store than the Society possessed ;
for subscriptions had been settled on a low scale. The

* See the Irish Literary Society, London.

projects of the Pan-Celts were retarded by much the
same causes as those which operated against their friends
in Southwark.

The growing strength of the Society could be measured
at the conversazione in celebration of its anniversary
which took place at Nassau Street on the 21st of March,
1889.   Miss Ellen O'Leary, Miss Rose Kavanagh, Miss
Teresa C. Boylan, Miss Maud Gonne, Dr. Hyde, Eugene
Davis, Dr. Pelly, T. S. Cleary, P. J. McCall and M.
D. Wyer were amongst the muster.   The latter's work
was nearly over ; a few months later he was borne to
an untimely grave.

In 1889 it was suggested by some members that a
well-known figure in the Irish world of letters should
be selected as President, and similar figures invited on
the Committee.   In this way it was thought that the
Society could speak with more authority upon Irish
intellectual questions, and protect the rights of Irish
authors in a manner hitherto unknown. Another section
was as strong for the selection of willing and practical
helpers.   The point was a nice one, but the fates were
against the figure-heads.   The majority very sensibly
decided that workers, and workers only, should have
the posts of honour.   In succeeding months they afforded
most disinterested assistance to young Irish writers, and
their work in the press did not sensibly diminish.
Amongst the foremost in the cause was Miss Ellen
O'Leary, though the shadow of death might almost
be said to be upon her.

" Lays and Lyrics of the Pan-Celtic Society " were
published towards the autumn of 1889.   The volume
was edited by Mr. A. R. Stritch, was in fact a private

undertaking of his ; and though containing some excellent lyrics was not a collection that can be fairly considered representative of Pan-Celtic poetical effort. It is marred by inferior matter, by a good deal which, the editor's statement notwithstanding, is not stamped with the individuality of the Celt. Dr. Hyde, Mr. Graves, Dr. Pelly, Dr. Downey, P. J. McCall, Mrs. and the Misses Sigerson, Miss Rose Kavanagh, Miss Ellen O'Leary, Eugene Davis, Miss Katharine Tynan, M. D. Wyer, L. E. O'Carroll, Miss Boylan, W. S. Burke and others were amongst the contributors.

It was the fate of the Pan-Celtic Society to see some of its worthiest servants snatched away by the rude hand of untimely death, to see others leave the old land on the track of fickle fortune. Most of these exiles we shall meet again. As for the rest, they are mainly to be found in the National Literary Society, Dublin ; in fact it may be said that the Pan-Celtic Society is still living in that promising organisation in which so much Irish intellectual hope is centred. In its day it began sterling work. It helped to show Irish men and women the treasures they possess in a long-growing, noble and distinctive Gaelic literature ; it showed them where their intellectual models were to be sought. It set young Irish writers on the true path : in their native fields, with the music and the appealing traditions of their own land around them. The rest was with themselves.

In 1888 came a notable addition to Irish literature in the " Poems and Ballads of Young Ireland,'' dedicated to John O'Leary and the Young Ireland Societies. Sweetness and fresh impulse rather than

E

the sign of robust intellectual personality characterised
the little book ; but it was readily welcomed as the
best of its kind since the " Spirit of the Nation."
Perhaps there was more finish about it, and on the
whole more suggestion of real poetry than in the other
nation-moulding volume.   T. W. Rolleston, W. B.
Yeats, Dr. Douglas Hyde and other singers who were
more or less strangers to the people were the lyrists who
now addressed Young Ireland.   Readers of Mr. W. H.
Hurlbert's "Ireland Under Coercion" (how fortunate
we have been as a nation in the foreigners who have
studied us, and given us moral lectures !) will remember
a reference to this book, and an account of a dinner at
Mr. Rolleston's in Delgany, when there were present
besides Mr. Hurlbert and the host, John O'Leary, Dr.
Sigerson and J. F. Taylor, the Dublin correspondent of
the *Manchester Guardian.*   Mr. Hurlbert, I think, found
himself in rather strong-minded company.   The " Poems
and Ballads " had just appeared, and were taken as
indicating a new inspiration in Ireland.   Mr. Rolleston
was in the "black books " just then, on account of a
pamphlet on boycotting, and certain strictures on some
aspects of the national movement.   Of his lofty ideals,
national spirit, and staunch integrity there was no question, but I scarcely think that he had grasped the full
nature of the difficulties and harassing circumstances
surrounding a less fortunate peasantry.   He said during
the evening that Ireland's salvation would be found in a
return to the principles of Thomas Davis.   In this he
was certainly right.   Three years after we find him
about to take part in a movement having that object
amongst the first in its programme.   The reader will

remember the reference at the close of the last chapter to a meeting at Mr. Yeats' house in Chiswick in December, 1891. The outcome of that meeting I have now to tell.

IV.

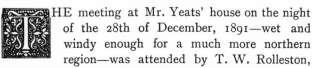

HE meeting at Mr. Yeats' house on the night of the 28th of December, 1891—wet and windy enough for a much more northern region—was attended by T. W. Rolleston, W. B. Yeats, D. J. O'Donoghue, Dr. Todhunter, J. G. O'Keeffe (late secretary of the Southwark Irish Literary Club), and the present writer. Francis A. Fahy and Thomas Boyd were prevented from attending owing to insufficient notice. The house seemed "beyant the beyants," as we say in Ireland, but when reached at last we had our reward, for it was in every sense a meet haunt for a poet or an artist. We soon forgot the taunts and rebuffs of old Boreas, wafted as we were by the associations and the conversation to the dreamland of an Irish Olympus. Yeats was full of schemes and projects: and I cannot say that the Southwark element was wanting in enthusiasm. We talked much about Rolleston's probable share in the work, before he arrived, which was somewhat late in the evening. He had already become well-known as a

T. W. ROLLESTON.

critic, a scholar, and an editor, but his Irish work for the *Dublin University Review* appealed more directly to our sympathies. The opinion was freely expressed by one who knew him that he had rather lost faith in such enterprises as we contemplated, but that if we could show him any reasonable hopes of success, his enthusiasm would be speedily rekindled, and the move-ment have no more resourceful supporter.

At length he entered, accompanied by his friend, Dr. Todhunter. The latter, though a most genial man, appeared a little hurt at the rude attentions of the elements—whose behaviour could scarcely have been worse—seeming like a would-be gentle Gaelic bard who was goaded into the writing of a tremendous satire. Rolleston, on the other hand, was calm as the veriest stoic. He who had held converse with the spirits of Epictetus and Plato was entirely unruffled by Boreas. One could not fail to be struck by his splendid physique, his refined, intellectual features, and his whole air of repose and suavity. One's first idea of him was that of a man of deep culture, searching thought, and superiority to common schemes and passions. It were easy to picture him as a dweller in Attic haunts, or entirely at home in an Athenian academy. Yet he had also an air of strength and courage which was, perhaps, more Roman than Greek. To Yeats, unmistakable Irish mystic, he was a curious contrast. Only once in the course of the evening did he show any trace of strong feeling—that was when some one, on a reference to Walt Whitman's illness, spoke in a somewhat depreci-atory fashion of the author of " Leaves of Grass." Rolleston was an enthusiastic believer in Whitman, and had, in conjunction with Dr. Knortz, translated " The Leaves " into German, of which language he is a master. He was, therefore, not at all disposed to let depreciation pass unchallenged, and spoke trenchantly, though briefly, for his favourite. Many Irish retrospects and prospects were indulged in that evening, Rolleston seeming at the time to be much more of the critic than the enthusiast. One could see that he was genuinely anxious for a movement to popularise or promote Irish literature, but he was not the less disposed to examine the initial ideas and the initial ground as with a microscope. The strong point started upon was the certain support of the Southwark people who were still in London.

Several plans were put forward. A central Irish literary club for London, meeting weekly or fortnightly, comprising every friendly Irish writer in London, good lectures on its programme, and a scheme for the publication and circulation of Irish books in the hands of its committee, was the favourite one. These books should in some cases be new, in others republications of forgotten or neglected Irish writers. There was no difference of opinion on the point that such a central society as was hoped for should be far more than a mere Irish club—that it could not flourish without, as it were, a missionary spirit—that it should also be, in some measure, creative—should possess an intellectual voice. Possible helpers were discussed, and those regarded as certain to join and to work were John Augustus O'Shea, Edmund Downey, Lionel Johnson, Mrs. Bryant, Barry O'Brien, Richard Dowling, Rev. Stopford Brooke, G. A. Greene, and others. J. G. O'Keeffe was appointed provisional secretary ; but this post was taken soon afterwards by Rolleston. Before the meeting broke up, a plan of campaign was discussed and decided on. This was the first of many meetings and discussions, held during the next few months in centres many miles apart. Some were in the Clapham Reform Club, others at the houses of J. G. O'Keeffe, Major McGuinness, Rolleston, F. A. Fahy, Edmund Downey, Barry O'Brien's chambers, and the " Cheshire Cheese " in Fleet Street. From city to suburb, and from suburb to city, were the weekly or other drives, till there was a general sigh for a permanent home. It was at the Clapham Reform Club, on January 13th, 1892, that it was formally decided to run an Irish Literary Society on the new lines. All those who had been suggested as supporters at the first meeting came in without hesitation, and several were to be met at the early re-unions. Amongst others, the most active was W. M. Crook, a young journalist and politician—a Trinity man, too ; one who was expected to render a good account of himself as an orator.

From the start the promise was decidedly good. Rolleston proved himself an enthusiast and a capable organiser. It was frequently remarked that he had at length found his proper Irish sphere. He was faithfully assisted by a dozen of the organisers, who found new friends in the cause week after week. We were able from the start to keep the question well before the public through the medium of the press. The following extracts from an article on the new departure by " One of the Members," in the *Freeman's Journal* of February 6th, 1892, may afford some idea of our early aims : –

" So much for the literary ' atmosphere.' The greatest hopes of the association are yet in another direction.
It aims to be above all things creative. Lectures, meetings, sympathy and atmosphere are really with it but
the means to an end. Having created the sympathetic
surroundings, it will wisely leave individual members to
the bent of their own powers, and the cultivation of
their own resources, but from the exercise of these it
hopes that the long neglected work of Young Ireland
will be resumed. It hopes that the unfinished schemes
of '42 and '45 will be taken up; the aspirations of '92
fitly voiced and chronicled as well. In fact already
certain original works suggested by the known capa-
bilities of some members have been talked of in connection with the programme. These books would deal
with matters of history, biography, poetry and folk-lore.
For the present I need only say of the contemplated
series that Ireland (or at any rate literary Ireland) has
been ripe for it this many a day. There are obviously
some other channels in which the Society may be
expected to work. Old editions and valuable books
out of print will be seen to, and arrangements will be
tried for bringing Irish books within easier reach of our
reading world in London. The Society has also in its
mind, in connection with home organisations of a
kindred nature, a scheme for the better and easier
distribution of books throughout Ireland. . . . It
welcomes every person of Irish sympathies and honest
literary tastes. It expects from every member both
earnest effort and the spirit of Young Irelandism. . . .
Here, then, with high hopes and vigorous aims the
Irish Literary Society, London, begins its career.

Home traditions and national ideas will be safe in its keeping. In the first place an intellectual centre, it may by its work add grace and brightness to Irish song; heart and life-blood it may impart to famished sections of our literature. As years pass on, and the literatures of other lands grow old and strong, and a proud possession to the people, the hoping Irish worker sees great things to be done for his own :—To mould into guise that will live some of the cold, great things of the dim past ; to gather together the hidden beauties upon old life by-ways ; to seek out the treasures of the present —crushed, neglected, or dormant as they too often lie— and touch them with the magic of the poet's art or the romancist's charming. Such are the high ideals of the kindred Irish spirits who have banded themselves together for thought and work in the heart of London. They have trust, and energy, and belief. Their Arcady is ' Ireland of the four bright seas.' Their muse is ' Dark Rosaleen.' "

There was naturally much talk about a new Irish Library (the Library of the Southwark Club, by the way, passed on with us as usual) at some of the initial gatherings. Certain necessary books were suggested, as well as the most capable men to write them. Several titles for the series were discussed, amongst them being " The Shamrock Library," " The National Library of Ireland," and " The Red Branch Library." Yeats believed that a good designation would be " The Bell-branch Library," there being, however, the one unfortunate disadvantage that the general public, being ignorant of Irish legendary lore, would not know the meaning of it. In reference to Irish books, a well-

known publisher had written to one of us some time
before :—" If my twelve or thirteen years' experience of
the publishing business is of any account, I should be
inclined to say that it would put another St. Patrick to
the pin of his collar to convert the Irish people into a
book-reading and book-buying nation." But under the
influence of the growing enthusiasm, and with the
prospect of improved means of distribution, more hopeful results were expected. This portion of the scheme
was, however, left in abeyance, owing to the fact, soon
after announced, that Sir Charles Gavan Duffy had a
similar scheme in contemplation. Once again it was
determined to make. way for Sir Charles. It had been
decided some time previously that he should be asked
to become President of the Society. He had consented
with alacrity, and now it appeared only courteous, if no
more, to await the unfolding of his publication plan.
It is interesting to consider what the young men would
have done, if under the spell of the new spirit, they had
gone to work upon their own lines. Some of them, such
as W. B. Yeats, have since published independent books
which, to put it mildly, challenge comparison with the
best in the old Library of Ireland.

We gained helpers every week in London—authors,
journalists, artists, civil servants, and doctors were
brought in by one organiser or another ; nor had we
long to wait for the tokens of a generous rivalry in the
good work on the part of our friends in Dublin. Of
that later. There was but one obvious danger ahead of
us—that a non-literary element would seize too much of
the reins of power, and hamper the literary organisers.
I must say that some of the non-literary members were

welcome, valuable, and self-sacrificing; but danger would
exist in the rule of others. On this account the election
of officers and committee at the inaugural general meeting, held at the Caledonian Hotel, Adelphi, on May
12th, 1892, was awaited with considerable interest. The
muster that evening, and the accounts furnished, did
much to prove that the Society, though still in the
homeless pilgrim state, had a future before it. A host
of friends were present. W. M. Crook presided over
a gathering which numbered T. W. Rolleston, John
Augustus O'Shea, F. A. Fahy, Edmund Downey, D. J.
O'Donoghue, Dr. Downey, Martin McDermott, J. F.
Hogan, Michael MacDonagh, Miss D'Esterre-Keeling,
and Miss O'Conor-Eccles. The Secretary had a series
of interesting letters to read from Irish public men, who
were in sympathy with our aims, and believed that the
time had come to test them. Amongst Irish M.P.'s,
William O'Brien, Justin McCarthy, and T. D. Sullivan
(who became Vice-Presidents) were represented. Projects and programmes were indicated, amidst a hopeful
show of Celtic zeal. For the Committee, the number
of nominations was rather formidable. Rolleston having
been chosen as Secretary, and Major McGuinness as
Treasurer, a ballot took place for the Committee, and the
following were elected : Dr. Todhunter, W. B. Yeats,
D. J. O'Donoghue, F. A. Fahy, J. G. O'Keeffe, Mrs.
Bryant, D.Sc., R. Barry O'Brien, Edmund Downey,
John Augustus O'Shea, Michael McDonagh, and the
present writer. Richard Dowling, J. F. Hogan, and
Charles Russell were subsequently co-opted, and the
present writer selected as Assistant-Secretary. An able
young Irishman, who had taken an active part in a

Dublin literary movement, speaking to me after the election, said :—" I see one danger, and one danger only before the Society. It is old fogeyism. Trample on it, crush it at every turn !" The words were the index of a very prevalent feeling that go-ahead policies and popular programmes should be tried. Fresh ground was to be broken, old furrows avoided.

For some time after the General Meeting matters went on much the same as before : we had the old order of round-the-city Committees, good organising (at which Rolleston was supreme as usual), and the consequent gain of new friends. At first it was hoped that the *raison d'être* of the Society would be eloquently put forward in June, when the Rev. Stopford Brooke would deliver the inaugural lecture. June, however, found London and the country whirling towards the maelstrom of a General Election, leaving literature severely alone. We decided to postpone the lecture to a time of less tension ; but the quiet organising proceeded as usual.

In June Sir C. G. Duffy came to London, in pursuance of various projects, and was soon brought in touch with some of those who had the programme in hand. Our feeling was one of pleasure and satisfaction at having the old Young Irelander in our midst at this stage of the campaign. Meeting Sir Charles soon after his arrival, I saw that old age had been laying rude hands upon him ; he was bent and weary ; he spoke in a pensive even plaintive tone; and in the hush of the lovely summer evening he seemed to turn to a world of shades and memories. Those who have studied the Irish movement of '42, and know the feelings with which young Irishmen regard it, will not wonder if I thought

he must have had a sorrow like Sir Bedivere's at the
passing of Arthur :—

> " For now I see the true old times are dead,
> When every morning brought a noble chance,
> And every chance brought out a noble knight.
> But now the whole Round Table is dissolved
> Which was an image of the mighty world,
> And I, the last, go forth companionless,
> And the days darken round me, and the years,
> Among new men, strange faces, other minds."

Sir Charles withal had still a keen and busy mind. It
would be a huge mistake to suppose that he did not live
as much in the present as in the past. He had missed
nothing in contemporary politics, and little in contemporary fiction and other departments of literature.
Though pressed with age, hours came which found
him equal to not a little work. He had pondered for
years upon Irish legislative and industrial problems.
Nor was literature entirely forgotten in his plans, though
very often it was literature of the didactic and ethical
kind. He burned with the desire, at a time when he
well might rest from his labours, to bring the benefit of
his foreign experiences to the service of his native
country. It was no easy task, for nations are often sensitive at the signs of such services, and in forty or fifty
years have grown into other ways, and developed complex policies. Thus it was, perhaps, that Sir Charles's
pamphlet, " A Fair Constitution for Ireland," though it
embodied the legislative and constructive wisdom and
experience of a life-time, did not receive the attention
which it merited. He was wise in turning to the
literary enthusiasts who, he saw, were a coming force.
By those in London he was welcomed, told their projects, and eagerly asked for details about his own. He

was inclined to defer his answer till some day when
he would be ready with every point, when a public
pronouncement could be made, and his wishes would go
forth to the general Irish audience. At the first consul-
tation between himself and the I. L. S. Committee, as
well as a few friends, held at his rooms off Park Lane
in July, the unfolding of Sir C.'s publication plan was
expected by everyone. The proverbial " time " had not
seemingly arrived, and generalities only were dealt in.
Mr. and Mrs. Henry Holliday kindly invited the
members of the Society to an " At Home " at their
residence, Oak Tree House, Hampstead, towards the
end of July, and here by arrangement Sir Charles was
to read a paper setting forth his ideas on what Irishmen
could do for Irish literature. The occasion was for
many reasons one to be remembered. The haunt was a
meet one wherein to gather and talk of literature. A
long way from the city dust and din, beyond green
lanes and hawthorned hedge-rows, amidst trees, idyllic
greenery, and artistic associations, it was in most ways
a contrast to the scenes amid which for years back we
had been planning for Irish progress. An imposing
number of members trooped in to the afternoon con-
ference. Sir C.'s paper was a notable one, some of its
interest arising from causes other than literary. The
old idea of helping on the industrial and national life of
Ireland loomed largely through it. He could name, he
said, a few writers worthy to succeed the men of '43,
but their work would speak for them. He preferred to
say that if there were not one man of genius left of the
Irish race, there were already materials sufficient to
furnish useful and delightful books for half-a-dozen

years. In proof of this he said that with a memory
running back over ten decades of reading, he could
affirm that there were scattered in magazines and
annuals, in luckless books overlooked in the hurry of
our political march, in publications the very names of
which were forgotten by the present generation, Irish
stories of surpassing interest, fit to win and fascinate
young Irish readers. In other domains of literature
Irish writers had carried their work to periodicals
wherein it had lain interred for generations. Continuing, he said that it would be presumptuous to name the
books which ought to be published, but they might
profitably consider the class and character to be preferred. The people would read picturesque biographies,
which are history individualised, or vivid sketches of
memorable eras, which are history vitalised. He
readily recognised the difficulty of reaching the people,
owing to the scarcity of Irish booksellers, but suggested
the adoption of a system of canvassing. The lecture
was highly optimistic and eloquent in parts. " In that
mystic clime," he said, " on the verge of the Western
horizon, where the more debasing currents of European
civilization only visit it at high tide, there is place for a
great experiment for humanity." This was a high key
to strike, but the Irish Literary Society regarded it as
the right one.

The central hope of all was the starting of a Limited
Liability Company to publish and distribute Irish books,
new and old. Only a general statement and a little
discussion were possible at a Saturday afternoon gathering, which already had been occupied with many topics.
There was no doubt, however, of the Society's support

—such a scheme was after its own heart ; from the initial stages this plan of not only publishing Irish books, but bringing them to the homes of the people was regarded as amongst the first articles of its mission. Nor was it needful to wait long for assurances and offers of support from the outside world. The response to the appeal and the idea was a quick and generous one. It looked as if the prompt success which attended the organising of the Society itself would attend that also of the proposed Publishing Company. The sympathies of a strong Irish element had apparently been touched ; it evidently believed that those within the movement had good to give, and it was ready to bless the givers. The Society was in the minds of outsiders closely identified, of course, with this publishing project. Without our full strength behind it, there was little hope of working it. The writers, too, and the organisers would be recruited largely from the ranks of the Society. This certainly was the thought of our own members when they gave in their adhesion to the design.

The time has not yet come for writing the full history —secret much of it is—of that projected Irish Publishing Co. of 1892. Coming to this part of our subject is coming to difficult and delicate ground, to matters on which some men who exerted all their energies to bring the cause to a successful issue entertain very decided feelings. Happily, however, in a general study of the Irish literary revival we have only a very incidental concern with these matters. As something in which wide-spread interest was centred at one time, in which generous enthusiasm was aroused, which was worked for with ardour and many sacrifices, and whose first

F

fruits were awaited as the most typical intellectual
offerings in the power of our writers to make, this publishing project cannot be ignored, painful though the end
was. After the Hampstead meeting a few men set to
work in earnest, resolved to take the tide at the flood.
Sir Charles Duffy was not alone in the work. For many
weeks two of the leaders in the Irish Literary Society
gave the principal share of their time and thought to it.
These were T. W. Rolleston, whose labours for the
Society have been noted more than once, and Edmund
Downey, the author of " Through Green Glasses."
Downey's services were necessarily invaluable, for in
addition to zeal for the furtherance of the good work, he
brought into the undertaking a lengthy publishing
experience, of a kind, too, which would be all-important
in the new venture. One of the founders of the firm of
Ward & Downey, launching Irish books was nothing
new to him. At this juncture he had retired from the
business, and literature was his undivided pursuit. His
hands were full of work when Sir C. G. Duffy broached
his scheme, but no man within the ken of the Society
was more fitted for the post of managing director than
he ; he was one of those regarded as indispensable. Sir
Charles Duffy shortly after the Hampstead reunion paid
a visit to Dublin to propound his scheme in the metropolis at home. The visit was not so satisfactory to him
as the London one. The Dublin National Literary
Society had got into working order, and a section in its
councils (including W. B. Yeats, who had gone over)
was more disposed to criticise Sir Charles's scheme and
its proposed working than their brethren in London.
They were the representatives of a new Irish generation,

keenly conscious of intellectual wants and wishes of its own, with pronounced ideas on the subject of their fulfilment. In a project in whose behalf they were expected to use pen and voice, and carry their Society, they wanted more control, more position, than seemingly were offered. Eventually, of course, the shareholders would settle several things that were at issue; but there was a feeling, or a fear, that Sir Charles, as Chairman of the Company, would be practically master in the matter of the new Irish books to be put forward. It has since been frequently said that Sir Charles returned from Ireland a changed man, his first faith in the idea not a little shaken. If this is so, he betrayed little trace of the change. For some time after his return all things apparently went well. His zeal, to all appearances, was greater than ever. One saw that he had set his heart on the design of giving again to the Irish people one series at least of what he was fond of describing as memorable and permanent books. This dream one could see had been the inspiration of years. The enthusiasm of the old is always pleasant ; in this instance, being tempered by knowledge and experience, it was so in a special degree. To friend after friend he went over the roll of his aims and hopes ; to sympathiser after sympathiser he told where the most effectual work could be done. Correspondence, interviews, and appointments were items which grew with the weeks. Rolleston and Downey laboured with the old zeal, the outside prospects were inviting, and few were able to remember a time when the press of either Ireland or England had given itself so much concern about Irish books and writers.

A Dublin element still remained irreconcilable. Mr.

W. B. Yeats opened a correspondence in the *Freeman's Journal*, in which exception was taken to what was evidently regarded as the one-man management of Sir C. G. Duffy. Some hard words were said on both sides, but some interesting points came out as well. Evidently the public interest was being sharpened in the question. The claim that the hopes and aspirations of the risen generation should not be ignored for antique reprints and Young Ireland aftermaths, was emphasized in several quarters.

The end came soon. At that time it was not called the end, but such it proved. Fate was against that particular Irish Publishing Company, though, in truth, few such projects had fairer prospects. Sir C. G. Duffy decided that he would postpone the project for a time. The provisional directors and secretary argued against this course, pointing out that the interest of the people was stirred; that Irish ability and enthusiasm were at the service of the Company; that it was strong financially; that seldom, in fact, had an Irish enterprise the chances of such favouring winds and tides. Sir Charles, however, was resolved to pursue his notion. He declared that public confidence was shaken in the business by the action of Mr. Yeats and others. It also seemed that active help would not be forthcoming from a certain Irish quarter—not literary, though—whence much had been expected by Sir Charles. There was some remarkable correspondence at this period, and a strange letter was written for the press, but never published. The I.L.S. as a body had no voice in the business, of course, —but its word was for work—not withdrawal or postponement.

Let us follow for awhile the further efforts of Sir Gavan Duffy in pursuance of his Irish literary scheme. Early in 1893 it became known that the plan of a Publishing Company had been definitely abandoned ; that Sir Charles was in treaty with a London publisher for the issue of his long-promised series of Irish books for the people. The names and writers of the first few volumes were announced later on. Sir Charles lectured to the Irish Literary Society in June, on " The Prospects of Irish Literature for the People," with occasional references to his scheme. The lecture was pointed and practical, but one noted that its tone was more subdued than that of the previous address. Sir C. declared afterwards that it was the last lecture of his life.

The first volume was to appear in September. When it was announced to be " The Patriot Parliament," by Thomas Davis, people said it would link the new literature interestingly with that of '42. In order to bring these books and others to the homes of the people, the writer formed and organised a scheme of colportage in Great Britain, Mr. Griffin O'Donoghue doing similar work in Ireland. Large sections of the people were expectant. The opening volume was awaited with the keenest interest. The opportunity of years had come. People generally associated the series with the Society itself, whose fame, as I shall show presently, had been sounded by press and public to the farthest ends of Britain. If the new volumes were worthy of the interest and the promises made, great was the intellectual good to be speedily wrought amongst the " sea-divided Gael."

The volumes announced or decided on in 1893, in addition to " The Patriot Parliament," were : " The Bog

of Stars," by Standish O'Grady ; " " The New Spirit of
the Nation," edited by Martin MacDermott ; " What
Small Nations have done for Humanity ;" by T. W.
Rolleston ; " Irish Missionaries," by Dr. Sigerson ;
" Owen Roe O'Neill," by J. F. Taylor ; " Dr. Doyle
(J. K. L.)," by Michael McDonagh ; " A Guide to Gaelic
Literature," by Dr. Douglas Hyde; " Latter-day Irish
Poetry," by W. B. Yeats; " Ulster and Ireland," by
John McGrath ; a new poem, also a " Life of Sarsfield,"
by Dr. Todhunter ; " Irish Songs and Airs," by A. P.
Graves ; Biographies of some representative Irishmen,
by D. J. O'Donoghue ; a volume on Irish Technical
Education, by Arnold Graves.   Mrs. E. M. Lynch
undertook to point an Irish moral through an adapta-
tion of a French novel, the present writer to edit a
collection of stories of the people, and to contribute
an original volume of Irish tales in the event of the
success of the series.   It will be noted that some of the
subjects were admirable, others not so by any means.
It must be added that in the early months Sir Charles
found it difficult to procure or obtain promises of the
best books.   Had he been able to do so, it is probable
that some others would never have appeared upon the
list.   Reviewers and leader-writers have occasionally
attributed the books to the Irish Literary Society.
The truth is that the President only is responsible for
the approval and issue of the Library items—the Society,
though it looks on all such ventures with a friendly
eye, and lends a friendly hand wherever it can, yet has
no control or voice in this matter.   It applauds the
energy and admires the enthusiasm of its President for
these books, but all the same they can hardly be called

typical of the contributions which it can and will make
to Irish literature. These remarks apply with much the
same force to the Dublin Society. But no matter what
other volumes may accompany or succeed the New
Irish Library of '93-4, we must always remember that it
helped to give a promising impetus to our national
literature.

Curious stories might be told of the movement for
popularising these books amongst the masses, for carrying them and others to ground where Irish books had
never gone before. This mission was in reality the
most important as well as the most difficult of all. In
the face of poverty at home, and in Britain one of the
most serious industrial crises of the century, the work of
winning readers in the Irish Highlands, by the furnaces
of the Black Country, the slums of Lancashire cities,
or the mining stations of Northumbria, was sometimes
a heart-wearing task; all the more so when the
organisers of the mission were already sufficiently
burdened with toils and risks. Yet the work of itself
had many keen rewards. It brought many proofs to
show that after decades of degrading and adverse
influences the Irish peasants had not lost their imaginative and intellectual cravings. We soon saw how to
work, and where, and how long we were destined to
wait for the harvest, which certainly would not come as
if by magic, however much we theorised in our easy
chairs or on our platforms. The people did not care
three straws for husks and shells, though we might call
them history, nor for morals however adroitly pointed,
and in their crushed, sordid-ringed lives they had not the
heart for industrial or statesmanlike problems. Some-

thing which brought back a little of the joys of old
times, the dew of Irish hills, the light of Irish hearths,
the bonfire's night, the merry Christmas, some wand
which waving showed them Rory's raids, or " Sarsfield's
Ride," which opened the gates of the faery world, or
whose touch brought the ghosts to the night-lands :
these appealed to them, as did anything fresh and glow-
ing with the new life and the new hopes of the old land,
whose songs, dreams and traditions had followed them
like guardian angels round the world.

Dealing with Sir Gavan Duffy's scheme has taken us
away from the growing I. L. S. In its new-found home
at Bloomsbury Mansion the long-deferred inaugural
lecture was delivered at the beginning of March, 1893,
by the Rev. Stopford Brooke. The fine muster and the
finer enthusiasm of that evening were tokens that the
Society had come to stay. The brightest names in the
worlds of Irish literature, art and journalism now
figured upon its rolls. It had found the light ; it was
already an organisation with *prestige*, and a mission to
fulfil. Mr. Brooke's masterly lecture, though it could
not, for reasons he explained, cover the. whole ground,
set high tasks and the promise of worthy achievements
before the band of workers. Impressing on them the
need and use of getting Irish literature into the English
tongue, he showed how they might prove their distinctive
national feeling, and the continuity of their national
being by showing that there has been a continuous
literature existing in Ireland from her beginning as a
nation, that from century to century it represented the
national feeling, that it had always been an individual
literature. If we wished to strengthen Irish nationality

we could not do better than make it largely rest on Irish Literature ; and that we had not done as yet.

"Translation, then," said Mr. Brooke, "is our business. We wish to get the ancient Irish literature well and statelily afloat on the world-wide ocean of the English language, so that it may be known and loved wherever the English language goes." Having traced the materials, age, and continuity of Irish literature from the Gaelic days, the lecturer commended to the Society "the duty of taking pains that this coming Ireland has ready to her hand all the materials for an Irish literature which will be written in English. Ireland will no doubt win material for such a literature out of her own fresher and more individual life, but new literature ought to be linked back to the old ; and the beautiful work of our country in the past will kindle her into the creation of beauty in the present." When we had got the old Gaelic stories into fine prose and verse, we may send, he said, another imaginative force on earth, which may (like Arthur's Tale) create poetry for another thousand years. Noble words like these from a critic of Mr. Brooke's reputation could not fail to produce a lasting effect upon the young Society. Dr. Douglas Hyde had a word to say for Gaelic literature through the medium of the Irish language. This speech, by the way, is credited with being the force which led to the formation later on of an Irish class in connection with the Society.* After toilsome days the Irish Literary Society was at last fairly launched ; it was now an organisation of national interest ; an argosy of Irish

* Conducted by Mr. T. J. Flannery, one of the leading Irish scholars of the day.

hopes and good wishes went with it. The publication later on of the inaugural lecture carried its hopes and purposes to distant scenes and students.

Other lecturers continued the work. Mr. A. P. Graves, Mr. Lionel Johnson, Mrs. Sophie Bryant D.Sc., Sir Charles Gavan Duffy (as already noted), Mr W. M. Crook, Miss D'Esterre-Keeling, Mr. T. W Rolleston and Mr. Justin McCarthy, M.P., reviewed their favourite fields of Irish life, thought, or achieve ment, in the course of 1893. Mr. Graves took up the work of Acting Secretary on Mr. Rolleston leaving for Dublin in the summer to manage the Irish Industries Association. As Assistant Secretary, Mr. D. J. O'Donoghue had by far the largest share of the Society's daily work. The members felt that Mr. Rolleston's unselfish services should not pass without recognition, and accordingly in December, 1893, there came one of the most interesting gatherings ever held under the auspices of the Society. Mr. Rolleston was entertained to a complimentary dinner at the Criterion Restaurant, and in the presence of the leading members of the Society, an address was read and a handsome presentation made to him. Some months before he had stated what had now become apparent to many—that the Irish Literary Society could not afford to stand still. It had succeeded beyond the highest hopes of its promoters, but it should continue to march forward and sow the seed in every promising tract. It could not rest from its labours until it had come into close and living contact with every Irish literary element in Britain, till it had effected the union of all the Irish intellectual forces in the country; till it had brought

them together for a great programme and inspired them
with new strength and vitality.

When Mr. Rolleston addressed the Society towards
the end of the year, but little progress had been made
in this direction. A suggestion to start Irish branches
of the Home Reading Union had been zealously taken
up by a section, but the results were not inspiring. On
the other hand, the Irish literary associations in the
provinces were ready and eager for federation with the
London body, but steps to meet their wishes, and ones
also to found kindred societies where needed, were un-
wisely postponed. Willing workers, towards the end of
'93 and the beginning of '94, were complaining that a
good working policy was not put forward. Compara-
tively little had been done to bring the various schools
and sections of the Society into one cohesive, vitalised,
and effective force. Still less had been done by the
Society towards drawing upon for any Irish purpose or
programme the strong intellectual materials within it.
The Society in the beginning of '94 had a force of nearly
four hundred members. A large proportion, as the next
chapter shows, had done special, some had done even
memorable work. Seeing the obvious possibilities of
such an association, contrasting them with the actuali-
ties as yet realised, it is little wonder that impatience
should ruffle the minds of the zealous. The Society was
now firmly established, there was danger in nothing but
in the failure to rise to the occasion, to fashion and
forward the policies of its founders, the programmes
that the people expected. The country looked to it
with trust and with hope : it dared not bury itself in
itself; it must travel in the light and onward. How

to make the most of its great capacities, of its wealth of resources, was now the problem. That problem cannot be solved in a day or a season. Help towards the solution is a duty of every member who has hopes and fears for Irish literature.

V.

E can better understand both the strength and the possibilities of the literary movement of our time after a study of the *littèrateurs* who compose and conduct the leading literary societies. Without a knowledge of their intellectual capacities and their Celtic ideals, we would be, after all, but travelling in the dark. I shall begin with one of the oldest figures in the movement — the President of the London Society. To many observers Sir Charles Duffy is one of the most typical representatives of the late departure. In truth, he is rather a figure from an old movement, who has been fascinated by and drawn to the present one. In Irish literary matters he is still essentially a Young Irelander; and the present movement, as we shall see, is by no means a mere later edition of Young Ireland. Half-a-century has almost passed away since Sir Charles first helped in the work of an Irish intellectual awakening. Since that period Ireland has been in large measure revolutionised; Sir Charles has gone meanwhile to the ends of the earth, led an active life, and returned to find another Irish generation in the old haunts, moulded by new circumstances, ardent with new aspirations. Another movement has begun, and grown strong. Sir Charles, as the representative of the older one, is welcomed to its councils. Before we comment any further upon this interesting junction, let us look more closely on his previous life and work, in order that we may more clearly understand him. He has had an exceedingly varied career, yet a few governing ideas have shaped and fashioned it throughout, Sir Charles clinging to them with the firmness of the typical Northern. Born in 1816, in the Co. Monaghan, he had in his youth, owing to family circumstances, a very uphill battle to fight. The struggle and its necessities developed his character, and had a lasting effect upon his nature. He managed to receive a tolerably fair education, though the Irish Catholics at that period had by no means even the educational opportunities which they now possess, imperfect as these are. Charles Duffy was then what he has been through his whole life, an omnivorous reader and a systematic note-taker. It may be remarked in passing that, in after years, even when Prime Minister of Victoria, he never allowed a day to pass without devoting at least four hours of it to reading.

In those school-days, too, he was a diligent student and gleaner of Ulster's history and traditions—traditions dating back to the troublous days beyond the " Plantation." (It is, by the way, a sore point with him that the history of this momentous event has not yet been written.) At an early age he drifted into journalism, and became the sub-editor of the Dublin *Morning Register*, to which afterwards two of the greatest friends

SIR CHARLES GAVAN DUFFY.

[Reproduced from "The Ballad Poetry of Ireland," thirty-ninth edition (1866), by kind permission of Messrs. James Duffy & Co., Ltd., Wellington Quay, Dublin.]

of his life, Thomas Davis and John Blake Dillon, were contributors. An important step in his upward career was the securing some time later of the editorship of the *Belfast Vindicator.* He also became proprietor of that journal, introducing to its pages features which were infrequent in those years in Irish journalism. He made the acquaintance of Dillon and Davis during a visit to Dublin, and in 1842 the three friends projected the *Nation.* Duffy, the Northern Catholic, found in Davis, the Southern Protestant, a man after his own heart. Duffy was the more practical and experienced man, Davis the more emotional and original. With the *Nation* a movement began, some effects of which are still a potent influence in Irish life. The " Library of Ireland," begun soon after, showed further the spirited stuff of which the young enthusiasts and their friends were made. A few volumes of the " Library " had suggestions of great things, but several of them, it must be admitted, were the merest beginnings of literature. Duffy was editor-in-chief, and his preface in 1843 to one volume, " The Ballad Poetry of Ireland," was the most notable piece of critical work he had as yet performed. The work of editing the *Nation* fell for the most part on him. Davis was the soul of the venture as Duffy was the skilled hand. Coming to his poetical contributions, it may be said that he was more of the ballad-writer than the poet, but though inequality was a characteristic of the Young Ireland literature, his writings must be taken as an exception. After the movement had sustained a severe shock in 1845, through the death of Davis, troublous days succeeded for the Young Irelanders, they were driven by circumstances into secession from O'Connell's party, and afterwards as Sir Charles pathetically says, " the famine swept away their labours." However, after Davis's death there was a rally of new talent to the *Nation*, " Speranza," afterwards Lady Wilde, being amongst the new contributors. In '48, the editor of the *Nation* was one of those who stepped to the dock for their opinions, but in his case the jury disagreed, and he was more fortunate, perhaps, than his fellows. In his "Young Ireland" and "Thomas Davis " he has given us some vivid impressions of those years. In 1852, he became a member of Parliament, and worked hard in the Tenant Right movement, the story of which is related in his " League of North and South." Some years before he had made the acquaintance of Carlyle, and was on terms of friendship with " the sage " till the latter's death. Those days are re-pictured in " Conversations with Carlyle," a kindly volume. In 1855, disheartened with home politics he emigrated to Australia, where his rise was rapid. In 1857 he was made minister of Public Works, in 1871 he became Prime Minister of Victoria, and was knighted in 1873. Some years since he retired from public life, and latterly has lived for the most part in Nice. His voice has been heard to advantage upon Irish questions on many occasions since his retirement. Though in some respects a stranger to the New Ireland, his long years' social and administrative experience in other lands gives his views a weight and an authority that are seldom called in question.

The dream of an Irish revival has haunted him for years. His idea of that revival is one whose effects would be largely industrial and social. He would see

G

the people profound students of the problems of Irish
history and Irish government; he would have them
grapple with the defects in their agricultural and industrial
systems; he would see them keen critics of statistical,
Parliamentary, and financial returns, as well as enlightened observers of their native resources. Every
Irishman should be a statist, a publicist, and a scientist
in a small way. Works of history and literature, tending
to clear up the difficulties of the past and sharpen and
train man's energies in the present, would also be
admitted to a place in the wide scheme. From this it
will be seen that Sir Charles carries his experiences as
a statesman into his dreams as a leader of a literary
movement. References to a higher system of agricul-
ture, and hints as to the production of marmalade, were
items in his first address to the Irish Literary Society;
yet so skilfully were they put that they hardly seemed
out of place. It must be admitted that for Ireland
generally, few things are more needful than a system of
national education more or less upon the lines laid down
by Sir Charles. In his capacity as director of the New
Irish Library he has taken care to include some works
that point these technical and industrial morals. It
requires much faith and courage to do so, as such works
are the aversion of the general reader. The foregoing
remarks will help to illustrate the interesting if somewhat peculiar position occupied by Sir Charles in the
movement. He is less of it than in it; and addressing
an assembly of *littèrateurs* he consciously or unconsciously
speaks as if he were addressing a Parliament or a
nation; with an audience not only of students and
scholars, but of agriculturists, bankers, manufacturers,

and Poor Law guardians; men who dream of main drainage, and men whose hearts are set on polytechnics. His view of the Irish scheme to which he is devoting the evening of his life, may be best described in his own words: "It is to begin another deliberate attempt to make of our Celtic people all they are fit to become—to increase knowledge among them, and lay its foundations deep and sure; to strengthen their convictions and enlarge their horizon; and to tend the flame of national pride, which with sincerity of purpose and fervour of soul, constitute the motive power of great enterprises." It is understood that he will contribute a study of Roger O'Moore to the Irish Library. His own autobiography he proposes should be his last work of a literary character. It is now in a fair way towards completion. Few men at the age of seventy-eight are as active and resourceful as Sir Charles. In his hale old age he is true to the hopes and traditions that fifty years ago made him a power in the Irish arena. The last works of his life are of a nature to gladden the spirit of Thomas Davis. When time shall have swept the differences and controversies of other years into "the gulph of bygone things," when his record in other lands is completely forgotten, we may confidently assume that Ireland will find in his Irish work—of the forties and the nineties—something which she may "not willingly let die."

Thomas William Rolleston is known to the outside world as a critic and a scholar, to the Irish Literary Society as a labourer of enthusiasm, tact, and ability, to his friends as a philosopher. In his thirty-seven years of life—he was born in Shinrone, King's Co. in

1857—he has studied much, thought more, and moved through other lands, gathering in as he went the best things in their literatures with all the zeal of the native scholar. A Trinity man, he soon outgrew the narrow traditions of T. C. D., showing during his editorship of the *Dublin University Review* that a robust Celtic personality was behind the work. He lived subsequently in London, and there again at a later period, after a stay of some years in Germany. Lessing, Plato, and Epictetus made a lasting impression on a mind already philosophic and plastic in a high degree. In his " Life of Lessing," and his introductions to Epictetus and Plato the depth of the study, the abiding benefits derived therefrom are easily traced. Meanwhile he was no stranger to Irish ideas. The reading some ten years ago of Standish O'Grady's " Heroic Ireland," was a turning point in his intellectual career. Like most of the studious young Irishmen of our time he came under the spell of Thomas Davis. A Nationalist in the best sense of the word, some characteristics of the Irish National movement a few years ago alarmed and disturbed him. Philosophic by nature, and academic by early training, certain traits of the popular revolution could not fail to excite not perhaps his aversion but his deep regret. In his claim for more tolerance, more education, more Celtic idealism, he carried with him the sympathy of all thinking Irishmen. Another personality that profoundly impressed him in those years was that of Wolfe Tone—in fact, he has made Tone the study of his life. Whitman, as I have already noted, won an early niche in his temple of favourites. We have seen already that in the work of the Irish Literary

WILLIAM O'BRIEN, M.P.

Society he appeared to find his real sphere of labour. He inspired confidence in all comers. People felt that they were not dealing with a scholastic entity, a literary problem, a professor of something or other, but with a man. Always calm, never ostentatious, avoiding the semblance of oratory as a thing unwholesome; spoiling his occasional speeches through an over-studious effort to prevent himself from saying what are commonly called "fine things," simple and sympathetic through everything, giving also the constant impression of sincerity of purpose and manly dignity, the dormant Celtic clannishness of the members came to the surface and rallied round him. Rolleston's work and character form one of the keys to the mystery of the Society's early success. Though removed to an engrossing field of labour—that of the Irish Industries' Association—his heart is as much as ever in the work. He is a man whose intellectual future it is difficult to conjecture, for, modest and averse to self-revelation as he is, we do not yet know his worth. From his culture, insight, and finely-balanced mind, it is not improbable that his work will be more critical than creative. If so it will be criticism in which much observation, truth, and life will be enshrined.

Though Mr. William O'Brien, M.P., is a Vice-President of the London Society, and was one of the first to applaud the idea of its establishment, circumstances have prevented him from being a constant supporter. I write about him here, rather than apart from the Irish Literary Society, partly because he is, in a curious degree, the opposite of Rolleston. The latter clings to classic traditions—William O'Brien is revo-

lutionary in this as in other things. Both men have
great force of character, which is exerted in almost
opposite directions. Rolleston has the philosopher's
idea of individual development and grasp of truth
—O'Brien identifies himself with a nation. Rolleston is
an Irishman moulded by Greek and German ideals,
longing to see Ireland in touch with the highest
outer humanity—the Member for Cork is an embodiment
of a world of Munster traits, intellectual, militant, and
imaginative. One is the representative of a Cult—the
other of a Cause. One typifies scholasticism and the
higher stoicism—the other is Celtic passion and power
personified. Rolleston has known in his life a good
deal of the scholar's calm and introspective happiness—
associating peace with William O'Brien's life would be
imitating the man who talked of sleeping in the bed of a
torrent, or in sheets of lightning. To much of his
career, with its daring, dramatic, and picturesque
associations, there has been a sad and stormy background. He comes of a family that has given many
devotees to the national cause. His brother, James
Nagle O'Brien, a prominent Fenian, is supposed to be
the original of Ken Rohan in " When We Were Boys."
The strenuous public part he played in the Land
League years was a touching contrast to his solitary
private life, several members of his family having been
snatched away by disease some years earlier. The
future historian will see that few men did more than he
to make and mould the Land League movement. As
editor of *United Ireland* he helped to rouse the helpless,
and sometimes slavish Irish peasant into a new man of
fiery energy and passion. His influence with the grow-

ing generation was scarcely less. He has carried his passionate Celtism into his books. His novels are war as well as literature. A critic has seen in the " Faery Queen " the epic of the English wars in Ireland ; and perhaps it was such from Spenser's point of view. " When We Were Boys " is also an epic and an apologia ; but this time the representative of the defending race tells the story, and points the moral. I know of no work that can be compared with it as an Irish national novel — not so much for its brilliant and poetical descriptions of Irish scenes, or even its delineation of admirable types of Irish character, but for the crystalisation in the conversations and discourses of the poetry of the national struggle. It is the revelation of the mission and the gospel which the sentiment of nationality has been to our Celtic people. A later book, " Irish Ideas," is a key to much in the latter-day inner life of the Celt. In short, in the present movement, William O'Brien stands amongst the ablest representatives of Celtic Ireland.

Edmund Downey has immortalised the humour of the Waterford peasant. Since coming to London in 1878 (at the age of twenty-two) he has brought that peasant on the literary stage in many moods and disguises. He trips across the deck in sea-stories, he is a 'land-smeller,' a chronicler of anchor-watch apparitions, an ancient mariner, or a modern ' or'nary seaman.' The author of " Through Green Glasses " and " Green as Grass " delights in the incongrous, and loves to play fantastic tricks before high history, especially that of Ireland. How often have we laughed at that king with the rope-tied crown, the man who had to brave the " Ordeal b y

Griddle," or that early British Sovereign who considered it extreme bad taste in a man not to don a fresh coat of white-wash every year! Those who have had the good fortune to hear such stories read by the author himself have carried away even more pleasant recollections of their fun and facetiousness. Downey is one of the most Irish of our recent writers. He has a full knowledge of the people; his peasants speak and act as we have known them to speak and act every day. The brogue, the characteristic twists and turns of expression, the happy-go-lucky airiness, the droll imaginativeness of local life he has caught up without the semblance of effort. This is only one side of his power. Weird shapes and cries have haunted us from his " House of Tears," shapes which his other books, wherein he brings us to a House of Laughter, cannot wholly drive away. He possesses the dramatic faculty in a high degree. His studies of Irish life have been far and away more searching than any of his books have yet revealed. Once in a while he will sketch for you in bold outline the sort of Irish novel which he would like to write. None of his published books could approach it. Kindling with the subject and the prospect he goes on and on till you must needs exclaim : " Why, this is the sort of Irish novel we have been waiting for this many a year." He will laugh and tell you that one cannot always select his best and favourite subjects. I have no doubt that given a real reading public in Ireland, and a fair field for a genuine Irish novelist, the author of " Through Green Glasses " might give us Irish fiction of a kind that would agitate readers and critics for a long time to come.

We have already recognised an old friend of the

movement in John Augustus O'Shea. No man is
more popular in the London Society than the "Irish
Bohemian," and certainly no man deserves his popularity
more. His nature is so many-sided that I despair of
doing him justice, as this book is not an encyclopædia.
I know no man who is so spirited an embodiment of so
many diverse traits. One morning he is a picturesque
journalist, enlightening his readers on complicated
questions of French or Italian policy; that evening he
is the impassioned advocate of Irish Nationality; a few
hours later you find him touching off the proofs of a
story of the Franco-Prussian War or of an essay on
Russian literature; anecdotes of Napoleon or a brilliant
lecture on the Irish drama occupy him next day, and a
later post may bring you the "acting edition" of his
new comedy, "with the author's blunt invitation to
laugh." He is a round-the-world historian, who draws
not upon a lively fancy, but upon actual experience for
his facts. Many changes have taken place since under-
neath the Devil's Bit in Tipperary he had those experiences of merry and dashing life which he has recounted
with effect in "Conal O'Rafferty" and other stories.
By the way, his sister in "Dark Rosaleen," a romance
of the Fenian movement, has furnished graphic pictures
of scene and life in North Tipperary. Mr. O'Shea is a
Catholic University man, with memories of Dr., afterwards Cardinal Newman. He was destined to come in
contact with a much higher dignatary of the Catholic
Church in after days. During the Papal troubles he
made a bold and successful journalistic stroke by inter-
viewing Pope Pius IX. Paris is perhaps the City from
whose life his memory draws the most teeming riches.

There he was the friend of John Mitchel, and others who in their time played stirring parts. Thère is a tradition to the effect that he went to Paris to study for the medical profession, but he admits that he is not competent to dissect a Norway rat. His volume " Leaves from the Life of a Special Correspondent " is brimful of anecdotes of these and later years of his. " Mated from the Morgue," a humorous novel from his pen, throws side-lights on other Parisian life-phases. Few men have extracted more of the essence of pleasantry out of life. He has described the serious and humorous sides of besieged Paris in " An Iron-Bound City " and in characteristic stories and lectures. Spain is familiar ground to him ; indeed, he discourses about the Continent as one might talk of one's native county. London has been his home for some years, though he has not neglected to visit Ireland, as readers of his " Roundabout Recollections " will remember. Though a charming *raconteur* and humorist, the laughter-moving art is not the greatest of his powers. He can wield English as he wills, and when he pleases is capable of as fine a flight of real oratory as any Irishman living can accomplish. He is the orator, *par excellence*, of the Irish Literary Society. Young writers find in him a fast friend but a pitilessly candid critic. A book containing all his " Irish Ideas " would be a memorable one. Within it we would find much that were pertinent to the present movement, for Mr. O'Shea's first thoughts of Irish revivals did not originate yesterday.

Richard Dowling is another Tipperary man, and one of the quiet supporters of the Irish Literary Society. He was an early associate of Thomas Sexton, Edmund

Leamy, and Edmund Downey; and, as in the case of
Mr. Sexton, the *Nation* office, Dublin, was his first
sphere of literary labour.   He has been in London
some twenty years, in the course of which time his
contributions to different departments of the literature of the day have been simply voluminous.   Entirely
averse to the crowd, or to anything like social recognition, he is still a stranger and a name to Irish London.
That his powers are fully and properly appreciated is a
doubtful question.   He has written graceful poems, but
is seldom spoken of as a poet; his " School Board
Essays " show a novel and quaint humour, but not
being the article which is known as the " New Humour,"
it has not brought him newspaper notoriety.   To some
readers he appeals most directly as an essayist—
" Ignorant Essays " and " Indolent Essays " have their
wide circle of admirers.   But in these days the essay
has fallen from its old high place.   As a novelist pure
and simple he takes a high rank.   He is a real story-
teller, with rich resources in the way of plot.   Mystery,
weirdness and morbidness he has made attractive half-a
hundred times.   It is not in his novels, however, that
we find all the charms of style of which he is master ; we
must turn to his essays to find them in graceful and
picturesque play.   It is frequently regretted that his
general work has lain so far apart from Irish ways ; that
in fact, since the publication of " The Mystery of
Killard," he has not written a really Irish novel, though
it is admitted that we often feel the Celtic heart and
trace the Celtic hand in his work, that with his fancy,
humour, and pathos he cannot be an alien to us.   I am
inclined to think that wherever he worked, the results

REV. STOPFORD BROOKE.

could not be strikingly different.   His tendency, though
he stood in the most Irish of fields, would be to drift
from actual life altogether, to revel in a world of his own
creations and imaginings.   Even in " The Mystery of
Killard," where scenes, movements, all things were
mainly in Ireland, there was not a great deal of Irish
life, colour, or character.   The author was absorbed in
an idea that led him far out from home life and home
paths.   In his best novels since, he has woven strange
plots and creations, planned extraordinary situations,
keeping local colour and actual life as subordinate
matters.   I do not doubt his ability to write a novel
that would be Irish in every sense, for he is much more
Irish and has a keener knowledge of our local life than
we sometimes think.   I wish we could encourage him
to make the experiment.   All the same, his province is
not so much the revelation and analysis of village
customs and gossip-natures, as the bringing to our midst
of secrets and mysteries from dark towers, blasted heaths,
and thrilling under-worlds.

The Rev. Stopford Brooke is so well-known as a
powerful force in several fields that it is wholly unnecessary to write of him at length in these pages.   A
native of Donegal, and a Trinity man, his labours have
lain in London for many years.   Conscientious motives
caused him to give up his living in the Church of
England.   He is now a Unitarian, and one of the most
popular preachers in London.   As a critic, an authority
on early English literature, an advanced thinker and
lecturer on social and industrial questions, his fame has
gone far.   " Riquet of the Tuft," a love drama (1880)
and " Poems " (1888) have brought him a reputation as

a poet of sustained power. Years of arduous labour in foreign spheres have not left his Irish spirit less warm. Amongst the busiest of men, he turned with enthusiasm to the Irish Literary Society in its early days of effort and project. I have noticed already the lofty programme, the fine spheres of labour, which he urged upon the members at the inaugural lecture. Ever since, he has watched its growth with liveliest interest, turning to give it a helping hand whenever the opportunity offered. Himself a man of striking energy and large capacities for work, his word has naturally been for the programme which must needs appeal to all that is strenuous and original in a society.

At the first meeting in connection with the Society, Mr. Yeats promised to secure the help of a young man who was then but a name to us. Soon after we had a taste of his intellectual quality in " The Book of the Rhymer's Club." In passing I may inform the Irish reader that the said " rhymers," who met now and then to recite and discuss their new poems over the social bowl in the " Cheshire Cheese " in Fleet Street, included a goodly proportion of Irishmen, amongst them W. B. Yeats, Dr. Todhunter, T. W. Rolleston, G. A. Greene, A. C. Hillier, and the subject of the present notice, Lionel Johnson. He was to the fore at the first general meeting, and made good suggestions. Later on he was elected on a literary sub-committee, and it did not take long for the guides of the Society to discover that a valuable recruit had been found. Whenever hard work was to be done, or a graceful, hopeful speech to be made, Johnson was ready for the task. Meanwhile his reputation had been growing in other quarters. His

critical articles and reviews were to be met with
frequently in the *Daily Chronicle*, *Academy*, *Speaker*, and
other London publications. He was probably the
youngest critic then associated with the leading organs
of the London press. Born in 1867, in Broadstairs, Kent,
but of a Dublin family, he was the first of a long line to
choose literature instead of arms. Educated first at
Winchester, afterwards at Oxford, he took the degree of
B.A. in 1890. It may be noted that in his College days
he numbered amongst his special friends the Rev.
William Barry, D.D. (of Dorchester, near Wallingford),
whose novel " The New Antigone " created such a
furore some years ago, and whose spirit is so decidedly
Celtic. Mr. Johnson became a Catholic some three
years since. He has a profound knowledge of religious
writers from St. Augustine to Cardinal Newman. Early
English and Elizabethan literature are two others of
his noted fields of study ; while Irish course-ways of
literature, it is hardly necessary to say, have not been
neglected by him. It is not every one who is learned in
the writings of the Fathers of the Church, and is at the
same time equally at home in discussing Michael
Drayton, William Blake, or the Irish Novelists. With
his slight, delicate frame and boyish face and figure, one
would never suspect Mr. Johnson of being the critic,
thinker and *littèrateur* which he is. A study of Thomas
Hardy is yet another of the critical labours he has
accomplished. In the second book of the Rhymers'
Club, he has a prominent place. It is safe to say that
he will be heard of ere long as a new poet. Though
amongst the youngest he is also amongst the ablest
pioneers of our literary movement.

ALFRED PERCEVAL GRAVES.

Dr. John Todhunter is another Dublin and Trinity man who first tempted fame through *Kottabos*. He studied in Paris and Vienna, practised as a doctor in Dublin in the seventies, and succeeded Professor Dowden as Professor of English Literature in Alexandra College. Neither medicine nor lecturing was exactly to his taste, he practically broke the connection in 1875, travelled abroad a good deal, and has since devoted himself to literature. Several of his plays and poems upon classical and idyllic subjects have revealed a rare poetic insight. He leads us round a world of dreams, legends, forest-songs, old tragedies and mysteries ; through a world sometimes antique, often haunting, often idyllic. Living in a mediæval century, he would probably have made experiments in astrology. When he turns to Irish subjects he generally selects a weird or passionate old legend. His " Banshee " and " The Fate of the Children of Lir " have set him in the first rank of Irish poets of our century. It has been justly said that he sings or chaunts his story in the style of one of the olden bards. He possesses the spirit and energy of the bards, and gives example very often of the wild, rough strength they possessed. He undertook a " Life of Sarsfield " for the New Irish Library. Now in his fifty-fifth year, his poetic powers at their best, full of faith himself in the mission of the Irish Literary Society, blessed, too, with ease and leisure, he is one of the writers from whom a great deal is reasonably expected.✿

Alfred Perceval Graves is so simple-hearted a man, has written so lovingly and happily of the Irish peasantry,

* His recent successful play, " The Black Cat," shows a marked new development of his powers

has been, in fact, so thoroughly at home with them as he
found them "cutting the turf," or "trotting to the fair,"
that one is inclined to wish that he had passed all his
life in studying them and singing of their ways. Given a
cosy cottage and a "snug" little farm somewhere in
Munster; fairs, patterns, markets, and dances of the
real old sort within easy reach of him, a Father O'Flynn,
an Irish fiddler like "O'Farrell," and "bosy" of the
true Munster stamp as his neighbours, his Irish songs
and pictures would have filled volumes by this time, and
might have united the best characteristics of Goldsmith, Kickham, and William Allingham. However, Mr.
Graves was born and trained in another sphere, and
amidst associations that were alien to the people. He
is the son of the Protestant Bishop of Limerick, was
born in Dublin in 1846, and educated at Windermere
and Trinity. Yet it was only when he turned to popular
fields and fancies in the south that he found his real
inspiration. Since he published his "Songs of Kil-
larney" over twenty years ago, he has done much work
as editor, dramatic critic, magazine contributor, School
Inspector, and writer and lecturer on school management; but his Irish lyrics, published and collected at
intervals, are the work that have come to stay with
Irish readers. "Irish Songs and Ballads," "Songs of
Old Ireland" (music by Professor Stanford), and
"Father O'Flynn and other Irish Lyrics" have appeared
since 1880. The work is not of uniform good; a man
who had so many business and official burdens as Mr.
Graves could not always be himself and strike his true
note. But these lays bring us a good deal of "the
light of our sky and the salt of our soil," as Davis sings.

When at their lightest they are polished and musical, and make good songs. Mr. Graves is careful to keep in touch with rural Ireland, and not many men are able to make as much as he of an Irish holiday. He comes back laden with anecdotes, merry experiences, happy recollections, quite ready to convince you that " a pleasant place is Erin," as the old song has it. On the subjects of Irish music and song he is an enthusiast; his labours to popularise them have been zealous and sustained. " Irish Songs and Airs " will be his contribution to Sir Gavan Duffy's Irish Library. At the starting of the London Society he was living in Taunton, but was made a Vice-President. Since then he has removed to Wimbledon, and has taken his part in its practical work.

The Society has several earnest lady members who have been prominent in its councils from the outset. Chief amongst them is Mrs. Sophie Bryant, D.Sc., who as the reader will remember, was amongst the lecturers at the Southwark Club. Mrs. Bryant has given many popular lectures, of an ethical or scholastic character, in London. She is a notable authority on educational questions and on the life, movements and ideals of ancient Ireland. Her study of " Celtic Ireland," published some years ago, did much towards clearing that antique ground, and affording the reader a clear insight into matters which were more or less confusing. I do not say that Irish students will agree with everything in the book, but there can be but one opinion as to the skilful manner in which the authoress grasped a difficult subject, the clear views she presented of its phases, the sympathy and the grace she brought to bear upon most

Mrs. Sophie Bryant, D.Sc.

points. She does much to keep Gaelic ideals and studies before the mind of the Society, and no one has more effectively emphasized the educational powers and mission of the Celt. In her lectures there is so much of grace, womanliness, and sympathy that the most inveterate opponent of women as public speakers would find his opposition considerably lessened after hearing her once or twice.

Francis A. Fahy has not quite continued upon his Southwark lines. He does his share of Committee work for the Society, and when he speaks does so to advantage, but we miss the lifeful spirit that launched programmes, formulated systems, and showed in plan and purpose so much tireless enthusiasm in other days. As a singer he has been all but silent for many a day. As a humorist he is little known, his best work in that department lying in the dreary durance of half-forgotten MSS. The sooner he is tempted to leave his poetic " Castle of Indolence " the better for the racy element in our native literature. Weaving " social lyrics "—real songs of the people—is his forte. They often seem simple at first but they grow upon us. The natural heart of the people throbs through them, something very dear and homely in Irish life finds expression therein. Such songs as " Galway Bay," " The Old Mother," " Irish Molly O ! " have all a pathetic spirit, an endearing tenderness that is of the people—

> So far away 'mid strangers cold she toiled for many a year,
> And no one heard the lonely sigh, or saw the silent tear.
> But letters fond the sea beyond would kind and constant go
> With gold won dear and words of cheer from Irish Molly O.

There are many pages of Irish life and history in that

verse. His love songs are also characteristic. They are not deep, but they are not imbued with any of the perplexing questioning, the strange philosophising of much latterday love poetry. They voice the love of simple, airy, but not unromantic life—such songs are they as the characters in Kickham's stories might be supposed to sing, and seem born for happy country ways and the heather and the sunshine. We would gladly have more of them.

Since the Southwark days D. J. O'Donoghue has gone steadily onward. For solid work he is without a rival in Irish London. While the Southwark Club was yet in existence he wrote in conjunction with Fahy an account of "Ireland in London," a promising example of research and industry. Just as the Literary Society had come into being he brought out the first part of his now widely-known "Dictionary of Irish poets," a masterpiece in its own way. It was a work which cost years of study and toil to accomplish. Hundreds of the writers had utterly passed from the Irish memory, and trooped back like risen Dead over O'Donoghue's pages. There was something spectral and grim about them, over many of them hanging a more touching interest than that which centres round those famished figures of old Fleet Street, of whom Johnson and Savage could tell stories, and who follow us like ghosts from English literary history. Yet the Irish student could not afford to ignore them; in cases where their work from the critic's point of view was unimportant, it afforded insight into the tendencies and circumstances of the time. The work was, in truth, a history in effect of Anglo-Irish literature—literature not only of the book

and the anthology, but of the magazine, the periodical
and the newspaper.   It deservedly raised the author at
once into a foremost place as an authority on Irish
literature, new and old.   O'Donoghue was then but a
young man, half-way or thereabouts in the twenties, but
with a long record of hard work and study to look back
upon.   Some years before his name was familiar to
readers of Irish periodical literature as a translator of
Beranger, Heine, and other Continental lights—there is
even a tradition that he dared original verses—but it
was not till the publication of the " Dictionary " that he
appeared in his favourite *rôle*.   When the third part
appeared in 1893, several thousand Irish poets had found
the light again.   Though carrying out this extraordinary
labour, and in constant correspondence with living poets
or friends and relatives of dead ones throughout Europe,
America, and Australia, he gave time and zeal ungrudg-
ingly to the work of the I. L. S.   Furthermore, he was
able to contribute to the press, to write for the " Dictionary of National Biography," to edit a volume of
Irish humour, and an anthology of Irish poetry from the
beginning of the century to our own time.   The two
latter works are in the press.   O'Donoghue has indeed
made a marvellous use of his years.   His Irish knowledge, singular and voluminous as it is, is only part of
his acquisitions.   He is master through self-study of
half the languages and literatures of Europe.   Of general
biography and history he has as ready a knowledge as
of the facts of contemporary politics.   Yet he seems
anything but merely bookish.   Slight and youthful-
looking, he is thoroughly Irish, vivacious, keen of per-
ception, and possesses a strong sense of humour.   Now

W. M. Crook, M.A.

and then he affects a delicate cynicism, and is master of
a happy art of characterisation. Though keeping in
touch with a large number of London Irish circles, his
centre of interest is perhaps the British Museum, whose
library, I believe, he considers worth the Seven Wonders
of the World. He is full of Irish projects, and has the
will and the way to convert them into achievements.

In William Montgomery Crook, M.A., the Irish
Literary Society found a young man who proved a
sage adviser and one of its most practical pioneers.
Mr. Crook is a Connaught man, who, like several prominent members of the Society, owes his training to
Trinity College. While under the guidance of the
" silent sister," he was anything but silent, for in the
course of his college career we find him taking honours
for oratory. For a couple of years before the starting
of the Society he was an active figure in London Liberal
circles, was a ready speaker, a clever debater, clear-
sighted and thorough in his views, and personally one
of the most tolerant and amiable of men. In 1892 he
stood in the Liberal interest for Wandsworth, and in
the height of a feverish election campaign came up
punctually from the toils of meeting and canvassing to
attend, like the most unpolitical, to the committee
business of the Society. At present he is the assistant
editor of the *Methodist Times*, and is studying for the
Bar. Flattering things are prophesied of him as a
politician. Though a man who has done much work,
he is still far from his highest level, and possesses a
fund of reserve power. Slight of build and frame, he
yet gives one the impression of abundant grit and great
earnestness. One's initial idea of him is that Nature

meant him at first for a fanatic, but changed her purpose and dowered him, in addition to strength and zeal, with a large store of reason, shrewdness of the keenest kind, and a pleasing stock of kindly traits to temper what otherwise would be an iron-strong character. Having heard one or two speeches from him, you are convinced that he has the wherewithal that makes the orator, and you wait the next speech with expectant interest. After hearing a dozen of his speeches, you are still awaiting that better something, but you are really convinced that a time will come when he will realise your high expectations. Given a fair spell of peace and ease from journalistic and political toils, he would find his full strength. Meanwhile he slaves away at committee work, organising, and routine—like a man whose heart is in his work for its own sake, and to whom the glamour of reputation is nothing.

Michael MacDonagh has been closely identified with the inner history of the Society. Just yet he has not the reputation which he deserves, his best work having appeared anonymously. He is a journalist—a journalist by birth and training as well as by instinct. He was reared in a journalistic atmosphere, and acquired a taste for type and printer's ink at a very early age, which taste has grown with his growth, and strengthened with his strength. His father, Michael O'Doherty Mac Donagh was a Donegal man who went to Limerick in his early manhood. For many years he held the post of foreman printer on the *Limerick Reporter* (the editor of which was Mr. Maurice Lenihan, M.R.I.A., the historian of Limerick), and was a man of some literary culture, for he published in 1882, a collection of poems called " Lays of Erin," which had a large circulation in Limerick. His third son, Michael, was born in the historic city by the Shannon on August 26th, 1860. At the age of thirteen he was taken from the Christian Brothers' Schools—where for some years previously he had carried off all the honours at the annual examinations—and became an apprentice to his father's trade. Like some of our ablest journalists he began at the lowest rung of the ladder, working up from the " case " of the compositor to some of the highest positions in a newspaper office. During his apprenticeship he was a frequent contributor of prose sketches and verse to the *Nation, Young Ireland*, and *Weekly News*. In 1880 he joined the *Munster News* as a reporter. One of his predecessors in this post, and an intimate friend of his father was John Francis O'Donnell, the poet, for whose memory Mr. MacDonagh and others have done so much, as already noted. In February, 1885, came a new success when he joined the staff of the *Freeman's Journal*, then edited by the late Mr. E. Dwyer Gray, M.P. Before leaving Limerick he was entertained to dinner by a large section of the citizens, and presented with an illuminated address. For seven years he was connected with the *Freeman*, during which period he filled the posts of reporter, special commissioner, leader writer, editor for a time of the evening and weekly editions, Parliamentary correspondent, etc. In the winter of 1885, one of those periodic failures of the potato crop which reduce the unfortunate peasantry of the West to starvation, occurred in Mayo, especially in the island of Achill. Mr. MacDonagh was sent as the Special Commissioner from the *Freeman* to inquire

MICHAEL MacDONAGH.

into the condition of affairs. His articles entitled
" How Things are in the West " gave some graphic and
pathetic pictures of life in Achill.

These articles led to the formation of a relief fund
which saved the islanders from destitution. When
MacDonagh subsequently visited the island with Mr.
James H. Tuke, the well-known Quaker philanthropist,
he received an enthusiastic reception, and an illuminated
address from priests and people was presented to him.
In the course of 1885, as representative of the *Freeman,*
he accompanied Lord Carnarvon (then Lord Lieu-
tenant) on a visit to the West, and again in the early
months of 1886, when acute distress was felt by the
peasantry of the congested districts he travelled through
the most remote parts of the country, writing several
series of articles, entitled " Life in West Donegal," " In
Kerry," " The Aran Islands," etc. As a result of these
and subsequent expeditions to the West of Ireland he
has obtained a unique knowledge of the social condition
of the inhabitants of " Darkest Ireland." Some of his
Western experiences were recounted in an interesting
article, " Life in Achill and Aran," which appeared in
the *Westminster Review* of August, 1890. Mr. Mac
Donagh also represented the *Freeman* during the Belfast
riots of 1886. Amongst his best work is a series of
sketches " Mr. Balfour at Home," which ran in the
Freeman's Journal in 1887, and afterwards had a large
sale in pamphlet form. In 1888 he was appointed
" Special Parliamentary Correspondent " of the *Freeman*
in succession to Mr. T. P. O'Connor, M.P., and during
the four years he held the post, his sketches were admitted to be amongst the best which ever appeared in

that journal. In 1890 he wrote another series of Connaught articles, and was through " Committee Room 15 " during the painful week which ended in the split in the Irish Parliamentary Party. His connection with the *Freeman* terminated in 1892, when he was appointed to a position on the Parliamentary Debates' staff. His varied and exciting journalistic career notwithstanding, he has found time to do good literary work for the newspapers and magazines. I may mention " Irish Graves in England " (1887-8—reprinted in book form), papers on " St. Patrick—a secular portrait of the National Apostle," and " Shamrockiana—gossip, grave and gay, about the National Emblem," (*Weekly Freeman,* 1890), " Thomas Davis : a Character Study " (1890), " In the Foot-prints of Robert Emmet " (*Evening Telegraph,* 1891), " Our Irish Portrait Gallery " (*Irish Society*); various Christmas stories for the Dublin papers, contributions to the Dictionary of National Biography, and a large number of articles and sketches contributed anonymously to the London morning, evening and weekly press. At present he is engaged on a study of Dr. Doyle (J.K.L.) for Sir C. G. Duffy's Irish Library. Full knowledge and a bright style carry him a long way. In addition to these he relies on great care and greater industry.

Mr. R. Barry O'Brien, the acting editor of the *Speaker,* is an able writer, and an authority on Irish Parliamentary and land questions. Much of his ability has been expended in studies that are foreign to the Irish reader. Devotion to rigid fact and aversion to the play of fancy are amongst his strong points. A lawyer by profession, the trace of the legal mind is

apparent in most of what he writes and says. His
opinions on matters of Irish literature and history may
be gathered from his essays on " The Best Hundred
Irish Books," reprinted from the columns of the
Freeman's Journal. His case is made out with much
skill, but the ancient, the unprofitable, and the dry-as-
dust have no small place in his Irish library. Getting
blood from the proverbial vegetable were almost as
likely an event as the finding of " sweetness and light,"
or the gleam of inspiration in some of those grim old
tomes. Mr. O'Brien would choke up the sparkling,
leaping mountain rill of Celtic fancy with forbidding
boulders and skeletons which he calls the materials of
history. He would crush Celtic Ireland under a cairn
of law-books, and then go forth in good faith to tell the
outside world of an Irish literary revival. Once, however, that you have come to understand this amiable
weakness of his, you will find him a good guide, who is
capable of affording a liberal deal of light and leading
upon baffling Irish questions. His " Fifty Years of
Concessions to Ireland," " Parliamentary History of the
Irish Land Question," " Life of Drummond," introduction to Wolfe Tone's Autobiography, and a number
of occasional Irish papers and articles, represent per-
severing researches and engrossing labour, in addition
to literary force and skill. As chairman of the committee, Mr. Barry O'Brien has been specially concerned
with the working of the Irish Literary Society. His
province has been to keep enthusiasm in check, to weigh
every suggestion in legal scales, and to put on the brake
at every indication of fast travelling. However, even
those who least agree with his ideas on the subject of

progress, must admire his devotedness to the Society
and to the policy which he deemed the wisest.

At our early meetings Thomas Boyd was a constant
attender. His work was entirely unknown to the
majority, but some of us who had read his poems in
manuscript recognised in him a real Irish poet. The
writing was of two kinds—the first charming but slightly
imitative, showing that he had walked with Keats, and
Herrick and Marlowe—the second distinctly Irish and
fanciful, sometimes quite original. He had all the
shrinking sensitiveness of the poet when poets were born
not made by their friends in the newspapers, as Mr.
Justin McCarthy says. Irish legend was his home
ground, and some lines " To the Lianhaun Shee " will
indicate his quality :—

> Where is thy lovely perilous abode ?
> In what strange phantom-land
> Glimmer the fairy turrets whereto rode
> The ill-starred poet band ?

> Say, in the Isle of Youth hast thou thy home,
> The sweetest singer there,
> Stealing on wingëd steed across the foam
> Thorough the moonlit air ?

> And by the gloomy peaks of Erigal,
> Haunted by storm and cloud,
> Wing past, and to thy lover there let fall
> His singing-robe and shroud ?

> Or, where the mists of bluebell float beneath
> The red-stems of the pine,
> And sunbeams strike thro' shadow, dost thou breathe
> The word that makes him thine ?

> Or, is thy palace entered thro' some cliff
> When radiant tides are full,
> And round thy lover's wandering, starlit skiff,
> Coil in luxurious lull ?

I

And would he, entering on the brimming flood,
  See caverns vast in height,
And diamond columns, crowned with leaf and bud,
  Glow in long lanes of light.

And there, the pearl of that great glittering shell
  Trembling, behold thee lone,
Now weaving in slow dance an awful spell,
  Now still upon thy throne ?

Thy beauty ! ah, the eyes that pierce him thro'
  Then melt as in a dream ;
The voice that sings the mysteries of the blue
  And all that Be and Seem !

Thy lovely motions answering to the rhyme
  That ancient Nature sings,
That keeps the stars in cadence for all time,
  And echoes thro' all things !

Whether he sees thee thus, or in his dreams,
  Thy light makes all lights dim ;
An aching solitude from henceforth seems
  The world of men to him.

Thy luring song, above the sensuous roar,
  He follows with delight,
Shutting behind him Life's last gloomy door,
  And fares into the Night.

Some of his poems, including the above, have appeared in *United Ireland*, but his chief work has yet to see the light.

Martin MacDermott is one of the last survivors of the Young Ireland era, and is chiefly known as the author of the lyrics, " Exiles Far Away " and " The Coolun," whose truth and tenderness have made and kept them favourites. Mr. MacDermott is now seventy years old. He represented the *Nation* in France in 1848, and in that year made one amongst the Irish deputation to Lamartine. An architect by profession, he served the Khedive of Egypt in that capacity, rebuilding

Alexandria after the bombardment. He entered with zeal into the projects of the Irish *litterateurs* in London, but in literature he is even more of the Young Irelander than Sir C. G. Duffy. The third volume of the latter's Irish Library—" The New Spirit of the Nation " was edited by Mr. Mac Dermott, who has also completed a volume, called " The Life and Letters of ' Mary ' of the *Nation.*" To the young men he seems what a gentle old bard of the bygone time might be after all the proud ones of his tribe had been gathered to their fathers—an Oisin with a kind, uncomplaining spirit.

Frank Mathew commenced an early literary career with a " Life " of his grand-uncle, the Irish apostle of temperance, and stepped nearer to fame in 1893 with a volume of Irish studies and stories, " At the Rising of the Moon." This book proved Mr. Mathew to be racy, observant and a good story-teller. It gave one the idea of an Irish author out for a real holiday in a region where he was very much at home—it had a good deal of the tourist spirit at its happiest—but something also which was in it gave promise of much better things to come when that holiday was ended and the writer had settled to more serious life. Mr. Mathew lately abandoned law for literature, and set himself to write a novel of Wexford in the days of '98.

I mentioned some pages back that several lady members have zealously served the Irish Literary Society. Some of them have made considerable headway on literary and journalistic lines. Miss Elsa D'Esterre-Keeling takes a prominent place as a novelist, " Appasionata," her latest work, being a pronounced· success. She has translated German songs, and writ-

ten plays and verses, much of which is original in
character. " In Thoughtland and in Dreamland," published in 1889, contained some Irish poetry. Contributions from her pen are to be met with in the *Leisure
Hour*, *Academy*, *Graphic*, *Belgravia*, *Temple Bar*, *Pall Mall
Gazette*, etc. Though born in Dublin, she was educated
in Germany, and hence it is, perhaps, that a foreign
atmosphere is over nearly all her work. This, however, does not detract from its distinctiveness and
interest.

Competent critics hailed Miss E. H. Hickey as a new
poetess some years ago. Those who have not read
" The Sculptor " or " Michael Villiers, Idealist " have
still to travel over some pleasant poetic courses, and to
walk with one who has taken a high and serious view of
life. Her first published poem appeared in *Cornhill*, and
others have been contributed to the *Irish Monthly* and
leading magazines and publications in London. Miss
Hickey was born near Enniscorthy, Co. Wexford, but
has lived in England for nearly a quarter of a century.

Miss Charlotte O'Conor-Eccles, who is a native of
the Co. Roscommon, has been particularly successful
within the past few years as a lady journalist in London.
She is now connected with a circle of leading women's
papers. Much of her work has been published anonymously, but poems and sketches have appeared over her
name or her initials in the *Irish Monthly*. Miss O'Conor-
Eccles has been from the outset a helpful personality
in the Irish Literary Society. Miss Eleanor Hull,
daughter of Professor Edward Hull, the eminent Irish
geologist, and grand-daughter of a poet, the Rev. J. D.
Hull, is another lady member who is coming to the

front as a critic. Miss Hull is on the staff of the *Literary World*, to which paper she contributes Irish matter. She possesses keen critical power, and has a pleasing style. She also takes rank as a lecturer. Miss Marie Belloc contributes to the *Pall Mall Gazette*, the *Sketch*, and other organs of the London world, and has done much general literary work. Miss Norma Borthwick, who is known as an artist, will be remembered by many readers in connection with exciting episodes of the Land War in Ireland.

The Society has some able lady members who are apart from its actual sphere of work. Mrs. Hinkson (Katharine Tynan) has caught the attention of the whole British and Irish reading worlds by her " Louise de la Valière," " Shamrocks," and later works. Her power is unquestioned, her nature is Irish, but her art and standpoint are sometimes English, strange to say. This is even evident in her Gaelic excursions. Yet poems like " Shameen Dhu " show a strain and a heart that are of the people,—our own people, simple and homely. Some of her religious poetry expresses the calm and the fervour of Irish faith. She bids fair to achieve with prose (much of it Irish) a success of the same high standard as that which attended her early poetry. She has not entered eagerly into the spirit of our present movement, preferring to work apart, and on her own lines. Mrs. Blundell, whose home is in Lancashire, writes much fiction and some poetry. Her novel, " Whither ? " published over her pseudonym of " M. E. Francis," made a stir of no transient kind a couple of years ago. Lady Wilde, who will always be associated with the Young Ireland movement, occa-

sionally enters the literary world in late days with a
book of Irish legends, or a volume of social studies.

Miss Charlotte Grace O'Brien has published some
volumes of Irish verse, and written a novel more Irish
called " Light and Shade." Mrs. E. M. Lynch also
tempts the fates of fiction, " The Boy-god " being her
latest offering. In " A Parish Providence " she has
made a peculiar experiment for Sir C. Duffy's Library.
Miss Hannah Lynch can be successful in fields of
fiction so far apart as those of Greece and Ireland.

Miss Alice Milligan, of Belfast, is known as the
authoress of many songs, of a novel, " A Royal
Democrat," and as part authoress of " Glimpses of
Erin." Perhaps her best efforts are to be found in the
Irish poems (somewhat unequal, however), which within
the last year or so have been contributed over a
nom-de-plume to the Irish press. Some of these are fine
work and give hope of finer. Lady Aberdeen, Mrs. E.
Crawford, Miss Maud Gonne and Mrs. Spencer Curwen
have reputations in others besides literary circles. Two
lady members died within the past year. One was Mrs.
Wynne, whose " Whisper ! " although the thought was
slight, revealed a real poetic nature, fresh, sensitive and
delicate. The other had been an interesting link with
the past. She was Miss Davis, no other than the sister
of Thomas Davis.

F. Norreys Connell is the pseudonym of Conal Holmes
O'Connell O'Riordan, the younger son of the late Daniel
O'Connell O'Riordan, Q.C., J.P., of Dublin and Cork.
Mr. Connell, who is one of the youngest literary men in
London, was born in Dublin and educated in Ireland
and abroad. He has been a contributor to many

periodicals and magazines, including such dissimilar publications as the *Westminster Review* and *The Stage;* and it was he who suggested the name of *The Speaker* for the well-known Liberal weekly. Mr. Connell has had considerable theatrical experience, his most noticeable success being the part of—what a facetious critic called " the direst villian in all Ibsen "—namely, Jacob Engshand, in " Ghosts." He is an enthusiastic supporter of the Independent Theatre and also of the new scheme for Sunday Popular Lectures. Almost simultaneously with the publication of this volume appears his new satirical work, " In the Green Park : or Half-pay Deities." He is also engaged on a novel. Biographical notices and portraits of him have appeared in the *The Star, Morning Leader,* etc. He is possessed of a merry wit and much power of satire and humour.

In addition to Rolleston, Yeats, Dr. Todhunter, and Lionel Johnson, the " Rhymers' Club " gave the Society some promising poets. Amongst them was George Arthur Greene, whose chief work as yet is " Italian Lyrists of To-day," published in 1893, and received with unanimous approval. Victor Plarr and A. C. Hillier were also attracted from the little Parnassus of the " Rhymers," and mean, I hope, to " hammer the ringing rhyme " on a Celtic anvil henceforward. The Hon. Roden Noel looked forth from haunts of Hellas, where he had found new magic, where " the gods survived with God above them," and the Irish element in his nature found something appealing in the new movement. He is not wholly a Greek or foreign devotee, for he has found inspiration in an Irish subject. When it was suggested that Oscar Wilde should be

invited to join the Society, one who knew him said that
he would certainly put off the matter with a quip or a
paradox, which, however, would be a good one, and
worthy of being entered in the minute-book. This
friend was a false prophet, for Oscar Fingal O'Flaherty
Wills Wilde was soon an honoured name on our register.
His brother, William Wilde, an old contributor to *Kottabos*, came also. The ranks of our poets were further
strengthened by Pakenham Beatty, the author of such
notable books as " Marcia " and " Three Women of
the People "; Charles Weekes, a young Trinity man,
who in " Reflections and Refractions," gave us work
sometimes faulty, sometimes imitative, but strong with
suggestions of not fully developed power ; W. G. Mart-
ley, another *Kottabos* contributor, Rev. M. P. Hickey, of
the late *Nation* circle, Frederick H. Trench, and H.
Quirke.

At an early stage we had a strong circle of journalists.
L. F. Austin had done much in the way of criticism ;
V. R. Mooney, now Reuter's Agent in Paris, could look
back upon stirring days as a special correspondent in
Constantinople and elsewhere ; Maurice Comerford was
editor of *The Stage ;* T. P. Gill had begun with a bright
weekly called *Tipperary*, and worked up *via United Ireland*
to the *Speaker* and other leading organs ; A. Hilliard
Atteridge had had a varied journalistic career, had been
on *Vanity Fair*, and was now the acting editor of *Picca-
dilly* as well as London editor of the *Catholic Times :*
William O'Malley has been manager of the *Star* and
National Press ; T. J. MacNamara edited the *School-
master ;* Edward O'Shaughnessy commenced with the
Kerry press, came to London, where he was appointed

sub-editor of the *National Press*, and afterwards London editor of the *Evening Press*. He acted as Correspondent of the *Irish News*, and in 1892, became sub-editor in the London office of the *Freeman's Journal*. Frank Mac Donagh served in the *Nation* office, wrote next for the London papers, joined the *Freeman* subsequently, and still later the *National Press*. He had ranged through every county in Ireland, taking care to investigate as he passed every trace or ruin of historical or antiquarian interest. He went on the staff of Mr. T. P. O'Connor's *Evening Sun* in 1893. S. J. Adair Fitzgerald wrote sketches *galore* and a voluminous world of verse. M. J. Callan, late of the Belfast *Morning News*, was on the Parliamentary Debates staff. Frederick W. Whyte is a publication editor, and a general journalist. He wrote for the old *Pall Mall Gazette*, Sell's Dictionary of the World's Press, and the Dictionary of National Biography. He is also connected with the country press. Alfred and Cecil Harmsworth represented *Answers*.

Justin McCarthy, Michael Davitt, Thomas Sexton, John Redmond, T. D. Sullivan, T. P. O'Connor, J. F. Hogan, Thomas Lough, Vesey Knox, James O'Kelly and Alfred Webb are members whom we may not pass over, though they have been more prominent by a long way in political fields than in those of the Irish Literary Society.

Novelists, better known in British than in Irish ways were drawn by degrees to our ranks. John Hill has several novels, such as " The Waters of Marah," to his credit; John Fogerty's " Countess Irene," and such books had more than the mere life of a season ; J. Fitzgerald Molloy gave us " A Modern Magician," and is a

very modern magician himself in the way of sensation-
alism ; Harold Frederic, a well-known journalist, in
" The Return of the O'Mahony," made an experiment
after Lever ; and Bram Stoker, Henry Irving's Manager,
found the materials for " The Snake's Pass " amongst
the hills of Connemara. Edward Garnett did clever
work on English lines.

The London Civil Service has been somehow a Lethe
of Irish intellect. Talented Irishmen who enter it are
in many cases lost to literature, or even the semblance
of literary effort, for ever after. This fate hangs over
even members of the Irish Literary Society. Certain
exceptions, however, must be made. J. J. Rossiter, the
first of them, was amongst the active members of the
Browning Society, published a volume of poems as far
back as 1873, and writes for the London press of to-day.
A second, James G. O'Keeffe has been a constant
working figure in the Society as well as in the Southwark
Club. He writes on such dissimilar subjects as Deirdre,
John Mitchel, the Brehon Laws, Edward Walsh and the
Gaelic note in Irish poetry. Daniel Mescal is another
such supporter who also came over from Southwark.

As these pages are devoted only to Irish literature, or
the signs of an Irish literary awakening, I can do no
more than glance at the strong force of professional
men, scientists and the like, who form an imposing
reserve in the Irish Literary Society. Astronomy is
represented by Sir Robert Ball ; Sir Charles Russell,
General P. A. Collins, General Sir Andrew Clark, and
Professor R. H. Thompson are Irish figures eminent in
very different walks of life ; the Rev. A. Boyd Carpenter is a distinguished lecturer ; the Rev. Euseby

MAJOR McGUINNESS.

Cleaver is amongst our Irish scholars (T. J. Flannery has been sketched in an earlier page); Goddard H. Orpen has translated work of Irish historical interest; G. Brinsley Lefanu (son of the author of "Shemus O'Brien,") and Francis Walker, R.H.A., are representatives of art; William Ludwig, genial and Irish of the Irish, has done most worthy work for our native song and music, while M. J. Murphy (poet and story-teller), Joseph O'Mara, Sherwin C. Richardson, G. P. Moore and A. L. Cowley, have worked in their own ways for the same good end; Dr. Mark Ryan is one of the Society's staunch promoters; Captain Rolleston is a writer on military subjects; Professor Rhys and Alfred Nutt, two of the Society's associates, are widely recognised as authorities in special fields of lore and science. This list of workers, capable and curiously diverse, might be prolonged through pages.

I have left over to this quiet corner towards the close a reference to one worker, who would deprecate any claim to special mention, but without whose record no history of the London Society would be complete. Those who have had occasion to closely follow the fortunes of the Society are emphatic in their testimony to the arduous and unostentatious labours of one man who week after week accomplished more toilsome work in its behalf than any casual observer could credit. This was the treasurer, Major McGuinness, whose hand was at the service of every department as well as his own. We saw in his nature some of the brightest and simplest of Irish traits, and had many opportunities of noting what a gain and a source of strength are such men to a movement.

Dr. Downey and Dr. Pelly are members who are much as we saw them in the Pan-Celtic days. John Denvir's chief work we shall note in the Liverpool pages. W. B. Yeats, Standish O'Grady, Dr. Douglas Hyde, John O'Leary and Edmund Leamy have been so much identified with Dublin that we may consider them with the Dublin National Literary Society. One other Dublin resident is a member who has the strongest claims upon Irish gratitude, and is in many ways a model to Irish students—Dr. P. W. Joyce. His work for Irish history, antiquities, music and legends has been sustained through decades. " The Origin and History of Irish Names of Places," " Ancient Irish Music," " Old Celtic Romances," and his recent Irish Histories have carried Irish knowledge and a warm Irish spirit to most scenes where the Celt has settled.

After this long study, is there the least necessity to dwell upon the worthiness of the cause whose spell brought such workers together ? And with such a union accomplished, is it any wonder that, as noted at the close of the last chapter, those who hoped for the highest should complain of neglected opportunities, of delay when great work was to be done ?

VI.

THE MOVEMENT IN DUBLIN.

ALREADY in dealing with the London Society, I have had occasion more than once to refer to the part played in Dublin by those who had banded themselves together in the National Literary Society. Dublin might be called a city of temporary Irish literary societies. They rise and die with perplexing regularity. The National Literary Society fortunately possessed the materials of endurance that were absent in too many others. Like the London Society it has not wholly perfected its programme, but it has sown wide the seeds of progress, and has wisely tried, and with success, to awaken intellectual life not only in the capital, but in other Irish centres near and far. The originators of the movement—in the summer of 1892—were W. B. Yeats and John T. Kelly. *United Ireland* by means of its literary tone and articles had done much to prepare the way for it. This literary departure of the paper was principally due to its new sub-editor, Mr. John McGrath. To the whole movement *United Ireland* has lent a helping hand, and—a fact

unique in Irish journalism—it has thereby attracted some
loyal contributors, and many readers, who have been
entirely opposed to its political beliefs. The first in-
formal meeting called to resume the work in Dublin was
held at Mr. John O'Leary's house, in Mountjoy Square.
Messrs. O'Leary, W. B. Yeats, John T. Kelly, P. J.
McCall and J. P. Quinn were amongst this opening
muster. There was a long discussion about the project
with some members of the Young Ireland League—a
political and literary organisation founded in 1891—but
it was decided to have the new organisation altogether
separate, and quite apart from politics. A meeting was
held in the Rotundo in June, 1892, to formally inaugurate
the National Literary Society. Dr. George Sigerson
(who was to take a leading part in the work) was in the
chair. Miss Maud Gonne, W. B. Yeats, the Chairman,
the Rev. T. A. Finlay, S. J., John O'Leary and John T.
Kelly explained and urged the new departure. The little
band of speakers was an illustration in a small way of
that Irish union and fusion for which the thoughtful in
the nation have so often hoped—

> " How every race and every creed
> Might be by love combined."

Dane, Norman and Celt were here represented, and
difficult it were to tell which was the most Irish. John
T. Kelly was appointed provisional secretary, and
matters soon made headway. " In recent years," began an
appeal issued by the provisional committee, " we have
heard much of the material needs of Ireland, and little
or nothing of her intellectual or literary. . . Without
an intellectual life of some kind we cannot long preserve

our nationality. Every Irish national movement of recent years has drawn a great portion of its power from the literary movement started by Davis, but that movement is over, and it is not possible to live for ever upon the past. A living Ireland must have a living literature." It went on to say that Ireland had no lack of literary power. There were Irishmen of eminence ready to help to build up her literature if they saw but the chance of finding readers in their own country. Hopeful words followed, setting forth the immediate work of the Society—the study of Irish literature, the circulation of national books to be written by Irish authors of distinction, the development of a programme which would bring the studious sections throughout Ireland into touch and into line with the central body. The workers aimed to work in a national field—their mission would be wide as their country. Lectures, kindred societies, reading rooms and lending libraries would be the means of spreading their thoughts and their advisings over Ireland.

From the first the Society had a band of devoted pioneers. Dr. Sigerson, W. B. Yeats, and John O'Leary were always in the ranks of the zealous. Dr. Douglas Hyde was ever ready for active duty. If the Council considered that a lecture was necessary to-day in Galway, to-morrow in Cork, and next week in Derry, they were promptly undertaken by the President. John McGrath, John T. Kelly, P. J. McCall, L. E. O'Carroll, W. O'Leary Curtis, John O'Mahony (late of Cork, now of the *Weekly Independent*), and Miss Mary Furlong were steady and prompt in their service. Richard Ashe King, Count Plunkett, J. F. Taylor, Q.C., Rev. J. F.

Hogan, of Maynooth College, Miss Alice Furlong, and others gave willing aid from time to time. Only a short period elapsed before it was seen that the organization had the wherewithal to advance and mould a real movement. In August, 1892, the inaugural lecture was delivered by Dr. Sigerson at the Ancient Concert Rooms, Sir Charles Gavan Duffy, then on his visit to Ireland (already noticed) being in the chair. The origin, environment and influence of Irish literature formed the subject of the Doctor's address—in all respects one worthy to be taken as indicative of the studies and lines to be pursued by the new association in the metropolis. Masterly though it was, the lectures that followed kept up the high record thus begun. In fact the feature that stands out boldly in the history of the Dublin Society is its series of lectures special and sustained in their excellence. The opening series delivered at the Leinster Lecture Hall in the first year of the Society's existence represent contributions which, if expanded and elaborated, would form the early volumes of a very needful and characteristic "New Irish Library." Dr. Hyde's "Necessity of De-Anglicising the Irish Nation" might almost be described as sensational in its effect. It certainly deserved to be so, going as it did to the heart of a national evil which was preying on Irish life like a cancer. Irish subjects no less important found interpreters in George Coffey, B.L., Father Finlay, S.J., Standish O'Grady, Richard Ashe King, Count Plunkett, and W. B. Yeats. The Society took care to keep its young supporters actively at work, including that strong element from the old Pan-Celtic Society which had rallied to it early. In its own rooms at

K

4, College Green, there were frequent meetings during
the first session, William Larminie, P. J. McCall, John
T. Kelly and others contributing special Irish papers.
That by McCall, entitled " In the Shadow of St.
Patrick's," full of curious lore and glimpses of an older
Dublin has recently appeared in book form.*

Meetings to further the aims of the Society were held
in different parts of the country, other societies were
affiliated, Irish books were distributed—Miss Maud
Gonne being especially zealous and generous in the pro-
motion of this portion of the work.   The part which was
taken by the Society in regard to Sir Gavan Duffy's
publishing project has already been described.

Thus it will be seen that the National Literary
Society made a spirited beginning.   It has greater
work before it, in the national capital and elsewhere.
It still looks to a whole nation as the sphere of its efforts.
It is true that in a war-worn, strife-embittered land like
the Ireland of yesterday, and much of the Ireland of
to-day, it was and will be no easy matter to make an
impression.   Unpleasant and unfortunate forces still
stand between such pioneers and large sections of the
people who are sensitive, or might be made so, to a
literary appeal.   With no organ of their own, and an
Irish press which, with honourable exceptions, has
slight knowledge of or sympathy with their work (and is
anything but an index of the better Ireland), the difficulties are made still greater.   But none of them are
insurmountable.   The Society of itself has the power to

* Sealy, Bryers & Walker, Middle Abbey Street, Dublin. (6*d*.).
The volume deals with Mangan, Father Meehan, O'Connell, Emmet,.
Major Sirr, " Zozimus," etc., etc.

break them down in time.   It is as strong intellectually, to say the least, as Young Ireland was, though
wanting, of course, the opportunities of the latter, and
lacking some of that missionary spirit which did more
than literary power to make a force of the *Nation's*
" brave young men."

The strength of the Society will be seen from a study
of its *litterateurs*.   Dr. Sigerson may well have the first
place.   He is the strong right hand of the movement in
Dublin to-day, but his labours for our national lore have
extended over some four decades.   " Erionnach " is an
honoured name with those who have followed the Irish
muse through our periodical literature since the fifties.
" The Poets and Poetry of Munster " (second series)
which saw the light in 1860, exhibited Dr. Sigerson's
powers as a Gaelic translator.   He commenced his
lyrical life at an early age, for we find him contributing
to the *Harp* in 1855, when he was only sixteen years old
(he was born near Strabane, Co. Tyrone in 1839).   In
his introduction to " The New Spirit of the Nation "
Martin MacDermott makes the singular statement that
the last well-defined period of the *Nation's* life terminated
in 1855.   The fact is that the *Nation* saw some of its
best days after that date, its volumes year after year
containing distinctive work.   Much of this was contributed by Dr. Sigerson.   He wrote a great deal also
for *The Irishman*; and here it may be noted that Irish
poetry and song which ought to be as familiar to our
minds as " The Spirit of the Nation " lie silent and
forgotten in the files of that newspaper.   Some of Dr.
Sigerson's work, too, is scattered through the pages of
Duffy's Hibernian Magazine.   The general Irish reader

knows him chiefly through the medium of anthologies,
yet knows after all but a fragment of his work. The
fine poem signed " Patrick Henry" in " Poems and
Ballads of Young Ireland " was from him. His prose
works deal with Irish land questions, political prisoners,
and other home subjects. One notable point in
connection with Irish literature which he has driven
home of late is the influence for good which the Danes,
their thought and literature exerted upon it in early
stages. He goes farther and maintains that the Danes
were much of an elevating force in Irish life. Most
Irish readers are inclined to question this at first, but
the Doctor's facts are not to be lightly thrust aside. The
Danish strain is strong in him, and he is proud of it.
We could well make room for many such Danes in
Ireland.

Mr. W. B. Yeats is one of our youngest writers. He
was born in Dublin in 1866. He is, however, of Sligo
family, and bids fair to immortalise that Connaught
county. He spent therein several years of his youth,
gathering from peasant lips its faery lore and traditions,
of which he was destined to make remarkable use in
after years. His school education was begun in London,
and completed in Dublin, but the study that moulded
him most of all was that of Celtic lore and legend.
When he was about twenty years old his name began to
grow familiar to readers of the *Irish Fireside** and one or
two other Dublin publications. Critical essays of a

---

* An Irish literary weekly, started early in the eighties, by the
proprietor of the *Freeman's Journal.* James Murphy, the novelist,
was its first editor. It did much to encourage young Irish writers,
and for a long time was really racy of the soil.

W. B. YEATS.

novel nature, and dreamy and fanciful poems were his contributions. He had a triumph in 1888, when his " Wanderings of Oisin " was published. Not only did the work reveal a new poetical personality, but it opened the gates of a new world of poetical materials. Mr. Yeats ranked henceforth as the most imaginative of Irish poets ; but his imagination had often the simple air of reality. Occasional extravagance there was, but it was in keeping with that faery domain of vision and phantasy where the young poet was most at home. He was soon a welcome guest to the columns of various exclusive publications. After four years came his second book of poetry, " The Countess Kathleen." Though meant to be as expressive of Christian Ireland as the earlier work was of Pagan Ireland, the measure of success was not as full as before. Presumably modern, the best part of the drama was that wherein the author lapsed back to the mystical and the elfin. On a stage of famine, plagues, and the schemes of demons, with one beautiful, womanly nature set against the general horror, there was scope for the grimmest tragedy. But Mr. Yeats could never awe us : his Mephistopheles would dream dreams, and speak the fairy tongue. Lyrics in the book proved his old power of effective charming. In 1893 he returned to his own ground, and gave us " Celtic Twilight," prose studies of dhouls, fairies, and visions, which it were as possible to describe in a few words as it were to put the magic of the " Midsummer's Night Dream " into a sonnet. Mr. Yeats has edited several books, but we forget them once we glance at his poems and Irish mysteries. Like the answered Fairy Call of Irish legends, there is no ignoring, no forgetting these latter.

Of his song we may say, as he himself has sung of the bell-branch : " All who heard it dreamed a little while." One of his characters, evidently after his own heart, says :—

> " I would go down and dwell among the *Sidhe**
> In their old, ever-busy, honeyed land."

The *Sidhe*, I think, have come to dwell with him. They are as real to him as the green grass to the more common sight, though people, he says, doubt this belief in the fairy kingdom, thinking, he adds, that he is merely trying to weave a forlorn piece of gilt thread into the dull grey worsted of this century. Critics have been concerned of late to know if he has not really done his best work, or if there is, or will be much in his poetry of the enduring kind. He will dream away and answer the questions eventually, with new books and visions. That he will be a great poet depends to a large extent on the possibility of his developing other characteristics to the same degree as that already attained by his imaginative faculty and power of vision. He must shake himself free from the passing craze of occultism and symbolism, and realise also that the universe is not tenanted solely by *soulths* and *sheogues*. Even now he has done much the finest poetical work of any of those in the present movement. If it is true as John Boyle O'Reilly sings that " the dreamer lives for ever," no one is more certain than he of immortality. Round the two chief regions in which he has travelled—the land of western legends, and the fairy sphere—it is not improbable that coming cycles of Irish song will be centred. The Irish Elysium

* Fairies, pronounced *Shee*.

will probably inspire the greater of the two.   In those
beautiful legends of Hy-Brazil and the West-Irish mythology as they are in effect—there are far finer possibilities
for literature than other writers have found in the story
of King Arthur and his Round Table.   It is to be hoped
that Mr. Yeats has not made his last excursion into this
immortal region—that much of the good work which
we may expect from him in the future will be inspired
by the Islands of Youth where the Irish Immortals

> " Shall not grow sad
> Or tired on any dawning morrow,
> Nor ever change, or feel the clutches
> Of grievous Time on his old crutches,
> Or fear the wild, grey osprey, Sorrow."

Mr. Standish O'Grady is verging towards his fiftieth
birthday, and some sixteen years have elapsed since he
published the first part of the " History of Ireland :
The Heroic Period," that fascinating and graphic work,
the reading of which made a turning point in the intellectual history of more than one leader in the present
movement.   That book alone, in a thinking and reading
Ireland, should have made Mr. O'Grady famous at once.
Yet years elapsed before the public gave much more
than a passing thought to his writings.   Meanwhile his
unrewarded labours went on in the fields of Irish romance
and history.   " Red Hugh's Captivity " appeared in
1889, and, barring a preface with unfortunate passages,
which Mr. O'Grady sincerely regrets, and a little West-
British bias and colour, is a volume to be cherished.
Withal the author's power and insight were appreciated
only by a narrow segment of the Irish reading circle ;
but with this his fame was secure.   A *littèrateur* in every

sense, he gradually gave himself up more and more to his favourite pursuit, and to the kindred one of journalism, relinquishing the Bar, which he had tried for some time. Amongst further labour was one volume of a " History of Ireland, critical and philosophical." Most of the felicitous writing included afterwards in " The Bog of Stars " was first published in special numbers of the Dublin *Daily Express*, with which paper he has long been connected. A Trinity man, he contributed verse to *Kottabos*, but has done better poetical work since his college days. Some political matter has come from his pen, but with that we have little concern. His " Story of Ireland," issued at the beginning of the present year, caused some disagreeable, some just, and some pointless controversy. Mr. O'Grady is more of the romancist than the historian. When he leaves the poetry of the heroic ages for modern periods, with the trail of political passions and class prejudices across them, he, a politician and a man of the classes, is not a sure-footed historian at all times. Even in " The Bog of Stars," he looked at things too often from the Pale standpoint. In the " Story of Ireland " he wrote much that is wholly unjustifiable.

Mr. O'Grady deserved some hard knocks for this " Story," but it was not easy to look on with patience whenever the punishment was administered by people who were completely ignorant of his higher work, and who were averse to giving him credit for anything. To understand him we must remember that he has been trained amidst associations both Protestant and anti-popular. (His father was rector of Castletown Berehaven, and he is connected with the family of Lord

Guillamore[*]). He is a *Daily Express* leader-writer and has some English ideas that are alien, to say the least, to Celtic Ireland. He has other peculiar aversions and prejudices. But all these things should not be emphasised over-much. A member of the Dublin Society has compared him to a stately tree with some knots and twists, which, however, do not mar either its grace or its stateliness. Irish romance (and to some extent Irish poetry) would seem to be his forte. In this field of labour he has done delightful and illuminating work, which deserves the most cordial recognition in Ireland or outside of it. He is steeped in the chronicles, narratives, histories and State papers of every period he describes—in this respect a worthy example to all our young writers. His politics or his peculiarities we cannot help ; against much in his modern history young readers have to be set on their guard; but his real literature—masterly, graphic, and so strangely rare in our Irish world—is a product to win and hold our enthusiasm. His kinsman, Standish Hayes O'Grady, though not identified with the movement, is a first figure now in the Irish literary world. His " Silva Gadelica " is one of the best additions made to our Gaelic legendary store since the days of O'Curry.

Dr. Douglas Hyde is not only a writer but a worker in the fullest sense. It is difficult to speak highly enough of his Irish labours, but, however one speaks of them he has the satisfaction of knowing that it is really of little moment, so widely are they already recognised.

---

[*] *Vide* D. J. O'Donoghue's " Dictionary of Irish Poets," a work to which I am indebted for some biographical dates and figures in this book.

DR. DOUGLAS HYDE.

Dr. Hyde in a quiet way some few years ago, when few people in western Ireland were thinking of intellectual movements, started an Irish revival on his own account, and wonderful is the measure of success he realised. The fortunate travellers in our local legends who parted with their brethren at dubious cross-roads, and after many days returned rich in adventure and achievement, were no more to be envied than Dr. Douglas Hyde. His parting with his brethren (brilliant some of them were did not take place at the country-cross of the legend, but at the portals of Trinity College. It is strange, but suggestive of more than hope for the future, how much old Trinity, the Catholic College, and the National School have fraternised in this movement.

From Trinity we may say Dr. Hyde went to the people. We all know the result—the quaint, racy, love-some, pathetic Gaelic world he has preserved and vivified for us. He shows us the older Ireland in all her moods, by hearth, and home, and field, ere yet she made way for the new. The Doctor's Irish folk collections and " Songs of the Connaught Bards " have helped to bring many of our people back to their Irish selves. His labours on behalf of the Irish language have been equally enthusiastic. He may be styled the leader of the Gaelic wing in our movement, and it will be well if all other sections are as earnestly and skilfully directed as his. Of the Gaelic League, founded last year to encourage the speaking and reading of the Irish language, he is president. He holds a similar office, as we have seen, in the National Literary Society. Dr. Hyde has for some time filled so large a place in the Irish literary world that unconsciously we have come to regard him as an older man than he really is. He is only thirty-four. Kilmactranny, Co. Sligo, is his birthplace, but he lives chiefly at French Park, Co. Roscommon. His course in Trinity College, where he received most of his education, was a singularly brilliant one. Poetical contributions from his pen have been frequent in the Irish press, over the well-known signature of " An Chraoibhinn Aoibhinn," but his poems in English form the least notable part of his work. Good judges pronounce his Gaelic poetry to be much more distinctive. He is filled with the spirit of the people. There are types of the Irish peasant with whom one feels at home the moment he first meets them—Irish homes, too, whose very look and air are suggestive at once of what F. A. Fahy calls—

" The cream of kindly welcome and the core of cordiality."

Dr. Hyde suggests all this. On the subject of the old tongue of the Gael he is an enthusiast. I believe that if he were hastening on with a reprieve to a friend on the steps of the gallows, he would be induced to stop on the way if some one appealed to him for the explanation of a Gaelic idiom, or for other light and leading on the subject of the ancient language. I noted at the beginning that he is essentially a worker. At the moment he has more than one Gaelic venture in hand, and his is not a hand to grow slow in such labours. His literary work represents, after all, but a fragment of his Irish services. He does not reserve his strength nor bottle up his Irish propagandism for an occasional book, lecture, or full-dress assembly. With him the desire to induce Irish people to be themselves—to cherish their own literature,

music, games, associations, traditions—to be a people
with nerve, dignity, initiative,—to wear the native garb
that suits them, not the cast-off clothes of the nation
they profess to despise—all this is with him a matter of
every-day effort and duty. He is a tireless organiser—
we might say an organiser of victory. Such men justify
and vivify our hope for Ireland—that better Ireland
which is seemingly beyond the ken or care of the newspaper. Beyond distraction, conflict and clamour, we
see such men pursuing their quiet and earnest missions,
we find them leavening the thought and stirring the
young blood of our generation, now linking that generation with a noble past, and now turning its seeing eyes
to all that is purest in the present. As we see them
thus, we are filled with new hope—we know that the
movement of which we in our sundered ways are the
humble ministers is striking its roots deeper into the
kindly Ireland to which we all incline—is merging out
from society and academy to the peasant's hearth and
the schoolboy's desk, and must needs be a permanent
and a potent influence.

William Larminie is working on similar literary lines
to Dr. Hyde's. "West-Irish Folk Tales," his latest
book, helps to do for outer what the Doctor did for
inner Connaught. The old West's awake here again.
The volume, a capital addition to our growing literature,
has meant some years of labour and trouble to Mr.
Larminie, who we may hope will go farther and fare as
well. Irish legend is no new ground to him, as proved
by his two volumes of poetry, "Glanlua" and "Fand."
He is a Mayo man, and about forty years of age. He
was in a Government office in London some years ago,

JOHN O'LEARY.

[From a Photograph by FREDERICK HOLLYER,
9, Pembroke Square, Kensington, Lo.:dón.]

but retired on a pension, and now lives in Bray, Co. Wicklow.

In literary Ireland John O'Leary is not the figure which he might be. Work which moved an earlier generation—and which is not yet a spent or a forgotten force with the " Men of the Old Guard "—is inaccessible to the younger ones, quietly buried as it is in the open tomb of the newspaper file. Virile, stern, startling sometimes in its candour, " each word direct as is a blow," it had a nobility of its own, typical of that fine old Roman rectitude which close friends recognised in the author's character, and to which even enemies have not always closed their eyes. The editor of the *Irish People* passed as a " felon " from the Irish stage in 1865, passed with a simple dignity and a ready acceptance of suffering for duty's sake, regarding the whole tragedy as something obvious and commonplace, disdaining the idea of seeing heroism or the epic touch in it. All this was characteristic of the man. Returning after twenty years of suffering and exile, he found the old order changed, and could not take kindly to the new. The literary movement, however, won his early adhesion,. and the Dublin Society especially has had no more constant counsellor. He stands out in keen contrast to some of the leaders. Dreams and the happy witchery of illusions (using the word in the highest sense) are foreign to him. The faery light, the Fata Morgana on the mountain heights, the glow, the dream-worlds, the ariel music that enable the true Celt to cheat Time of so much of his dreariness do not shine or sing for him. He would not that they might. Sober vision and rigid reality are more in his esteem. Browning, in one of his later poems, looks back to the "alien glow" which in youth touched all things, and mourns that in old age it is gone—man, bird, beast are simply bird, beast, man. Mr. O'Leary would regard this as a blessing. The glamour of the Gael is unknown to him. His consequent clear, cold sight differentiates him from the majority of his comrades. His memoirs, now completed, will prove in all likelihood to be one of the most candid and striking works of our time. It goes back to Young Ireland, treating of Young Irelanders of whom we will gladly learn more. It is needless to say how eagerly the students of the Fenian movement await it. Mr. O'Leary will probably tell us much about the intellectual side of that movement—which is far more interesting than we sometimes imagine.❋

It is a pity that Edmund Leamy has not fared further in that world of delicate and delightful imaginings which he opened some years ago with his "Irish Fairy Tales." A real poet and a real Gael it was who summoned back those charming fairy presences to Irish haunts. When superior people talk about the Irish intellectual poverty of the last decade, or wonder where the new literature is to come from, this is one of the works to show and silence them. As editor of *United Ireland*, Mr. Leamy in days of painful politics kept many a bright corner for Irish *litterateurs*. Like others of that able circle (including Richard Dowling, Edmund Downey, and Thomas Sexton) in which he moved years ago in Waterford, he has written some poetry, generally on Irish themes.

Two lady members of the Society have taken promi-

❋ D. J. O'Donoghue, in some papers on " The Literature of '67," n the *Shamrock* (1893), has dwelt on this point.

L

nent places in the world of letters within the last year
or thereabouts. Miss Jane Barlow's "Irish Idylls" are
a luminous index to young Irish authors of that world
of appealing humanity which is still to be found by observant eyes in Irish local life. The fact cannot be too often
emphasised that there is an Irish rural world with vivid
and quaint interests entirely neglected by our novelists.
The vanithee, the "ballat-singer," the parish poet, the
village   statesman,   the   cup-tosser,   the   ghost-land
chronicler, the blind fiddler and a dozen such characters
are stranger to our fiction than they ought to be. Miss
Barlow's profitable excursion to one quarter of this area
has had results that may well lead others to make further
explorations. While Rolleston was editing the *Dublin
University Review* her first poem came to him anonymously. He was at once struck with its power, but the
"brogue" did not wholly pass muster. Several such
pieces were afterwards given to the world in "Bogland
Studies" (1892). Irish writers whose early attempts are
scorned of some critics may take courage from the
example and fate of this first offering. *United Ireland*
welcomed it, and saw its promise ; but several critics
could make nothing of it. They shrugged their shoulders
over the "brogue" and the whole form, confessed their
inability to read it, and cast it away. Afterwards when
"Irish Idylls" had made a stir, and the "studies" were
brought up again on the strength of it they found a less
frosty audience. Miss Barlow now finds herself amongst
our foremost writers, with every encouragement to go on
and prosper. She lives at Raheny, Co. Dublin, where
her father (a T.C.D. man) is vicar. Miss Dora Sigerson is the other lady to whose progress I have made

RICHARD ASHE KING.

reference. Her " Verses " is an unequal book, with
fibre, philosophy, fretful introspection, " storm-and
doubt " unrest, and much which is plainly poetry.
Moods not common with the Irish muse are represented,
also moods which are common, though Miss Sigerson
does not make them as poetical as the others. Her
sister, Miss Hester Sigerson, is a fugitive contributor to
poetical corners of the Irish and American press, and
fills Rose Kavanagh's place on the *Weekly Freeman.* The
Misses Furlong work for the Society, but only write
occasionally. Of other lady members, Miss Milligan
we have met already, Miss M. E. Kennedy's work is
now as it was for the Pan-Celtic Society; Miss Mary
Banim, daughter of Michael Banim, is authoress of an
exhaustive book, " Here and There through Ireland ; "
Miss L. Kelly has composed some Irish music ; while
Miss Teresa Rooney has published several stories over
the pseudonym of " Eblana." Some of them deal with
ancient Ireland, and are learned productions, perhaps
too much so. Mr. Aubrey De Vere justly says that
poetry refuses to take up more philosophy than it can
hold in solution ; and I think it can be said quite as
justly that real romance refuses to take up more history
than it can hold in solution. Miss Rooney has not
always kept this truth in view.

Lately Miss Nesta Higginson (Moira O'Neill), another
young Irish authoress—though outside the Society—has
become familiar to a circle of readers through pretty
poems and sketches in *Blackwood's Magazine.* Antrim is
her ground of inspiration. " An Elf Errant," an Irish
fairy tale from her pen, is promised for early publication.

We have still to meet some of the ablest members of

the Dublin Society. Richard Ashe King is one of them. Outsiders know him well as a critic and a novelist; the Society has had special experience of him in the *rôle* of lecturer. Few other members can discharge this function as brilliantly. He is intensely Celtic, but too candid to overlook the Celt's failings, as the Society is well aware. Since he gave up his living in the Church of England some years ago, he has devoted his powers to criticism and fiction. *Truth* has had keen critical studies from his pen, and a couple of years since he wrote Irish literary papers for the *Freeman's Journal* over the signature of " Fergus." As " Basil " in *Cornhill* he became famous with " The Wearing of the Green," a story of the Land League. Readers will not readily forget its clever characterisation, or the animated conversations wherein the " case of Ireland " is stated anew, and with bracing effect. Irish and other novels have followed this success, though at long intervals. Mr. King, we feel sure, is no more than in the midst of his best period.

I have noted something of John McGrath's work in the columns of *United Ireland.* He was only a short time on the paper when (it was early in 1891) he proposed to Mr. Leamy, then editor, that they should make it literary. At this period of the fiercest political stress it was only a man whose heart was in Irish literary advancement that could think of such a proposal. Mr. Leamy agreed to it, and thence forward *United Ireland* had many bright columns that were refreshing reading to friends and foes alike. Several of the men who were notable in both societies figured from time to time in its pages. McGrath, besides his labours in the paper did work, sometimes of an active nature, for the National Literary

Society. He had reached his twenty-seventh year whe
he joined *United Ireland*. The previous four were spent
on the staff of the *Freeman's Journal*, and still earlier his
poems (signed " Cuan ") were to be met with in *Young
Ireland*. They gave little evidence of the full Irish spirit
which he was to develope later on. Indeed in an
interesting sketch of his dead friend, Patrick Mac-
Manus, contributed about September, 1886, to *Young
Ireland*, he makes note of the fact that while he went to
far foreign quarters for his materials, MacManus found
happy success in the racy northern life at his door.
(They were both of Portaferry). As " Slieve Donard "
(he was also " Innishowen "), MacManus was a favourite with readers of the popular Dublin papers. A young
carpenter, as he worked at his trade he sang songs, and
in his leisure hours he penned stories, both of which
gave as much promise of living work to come as those
of any young writer in the last decade. He tried his
luck in America, but his quest was not long, for he died
early in 1886. Cut away in his young manhood he yet
left lyrics which ought to be remembered. His friend
McGrath soon found his more fitting field in prose.
Besides the journalistic labours I have noted there is
still to be set to his credit some notable articles contributed to the *Westminster Review*. In *United Ireland*
—or at any rate in its Irish literary departments—
he found his sphere of congenial labour. In difficult
days and circumstances he made a great deal of it.
He was not always serious, even when dealing with
Irish literature, and a stern censor might lay some
literary venial sins to his charge. The nearer he steers
to real literature the more natural and characteristic

JOHN McGRATH

seems his writing. He contributes an historical study, " Ulster and Ireland " to Sir Charles Duffy's Library. The subject is one to tempt an ambitious man, one also to put any man's strength to a severe strain, for Ulster's Irish record means half the history of Ireland.

Count Plunkett (" Killeen ") has written poetry of a high order of merit. Some of it will be found in the *Irish Monthly*—that medium through which we have received not a little that ought to be permanent in our literature. Much more of it is scattered over Irish and American newspapers. Still other examples of Count Plunkett's work may be traced in *Hibernia*, which he edited. Unfortunately too much of his happiest poetry remains uncollected. His one published volume, " God's Chosen Festival " (1877) brought him new admirers, but the circle ought to be larger.

Father Finlay is well known in Dublin as an editor and a lecturer, while outsiders made his acquaintance long since as the author of an historical story, " The Chances of War." In the Dublin Society he has several clerical colleagues. Maynooth has sent the Rev. J. F. Hogan, a worker of the most earnest type, and the Rev. Eugene O'Growney, whose name is now a household word with Irish scholars. Another helper is the Rev. Edmund Hogan, familiar to readers of the *Month* and such high-class periodicals. It is pleasant to note that outside the Society, too, the Irish priests are setting to work in new literary fields. Quite recently Father O'Donoghue, of Ardfert, gave us the story of St. Brendan, Father Fahey, a valuable Western study, Father White, the history of Clare and the Dalcassians, while Father Healy did much the same for Kilkenny.

Father O'Laverty has an honoured place amongst Irish antiquarians. May many such labourers arise amongst the Irish priesthood. Going higher, amongst the Irish episcopacy, we see the Most Rev. Dr. Healy and the Most Rev. Dr. Sheehan leading the way in historical and archæological labours. In kindred fields kindred labours by other ecclesiastics are happily beginning or proceeding.

Returning to the Dublin Society, we find George Coffey winning honours in Irish archæological pursuits, W. J. Doherty conducting Ulster historical researches, while L. E. O'Carroll, and R. J. O'Mulrenin labour as they laboured for the Pan-Celtic Society. P. J. McCall continues his racy offerings in song and story, sometimes over his old pseudonym of "Cavellus." John T. Kelly is a worker as ever, but not a singer in these days. Some evil Irish spirit has thrown " the cold chain of silence " over his militant muse. J. F. Taylor, Q.C., the Dublin correspondent of the *Manchester Guardian* has been prominent now and then in the councils of the Society, is regarded as a strong but independent personality, and will deal with the stronger personality of Owen Roe O'Neill for the " New Irish Library." W. P. Coyne has been another prominent pioneer and ranks high as an Irish pressman. W. O'Leary Curtis and John O'Mahony are doing good things in the same direction, and like others just mentioned are spoken of as two of the men of the future. Mr. T. Griffin O'Donoghue, with all his intellectual leanings and acquirements has had as yet but very slight opportunities for literary excursions. But his time, I think, is coming.

Such then are the pioneers of the movement in the capital. Surely in their work and their enthusiasm there is more than the promise of good for our new Ireland.

VII.

At Home and Abroad.

T would be a great mistake to suppose that the full strength of the literary movement lies in the two leading societies of Dublin and London. They certainly hold an imposing muster ot Irish *littèrateurs*,ꟼ but even they have something to learn in the way of resolute work and an ardent missionary spirit from some of the kindred societies in the provinces. We have heard that the Athenians understood what was good, but the Lacedæmonians practiced it. Some of our friends in distant Irish centres are also quicker to practice than their brethren in the big capitals; and let us not forget it. The efforts they have made have been against great odds; but after many years they strive on the old lines as eagerly as ever.

For ten years the Belfast Young Ireland Society has been a virile Celtic centre in the northern capital. It has had an essentially missionary career, and is justly looked back to as a national Alma Mater by many.

Its influence has been felt throughout Ulster. The
northern province has played memorable parts in the
making of Irish history : its wealth of national inspiration
and traditions comes home with appealing force to
generation after generation of young Irishmen. Belfast
itself, just a century ago, was the centre of extreme
national opinion in Ireland. The Young Ireland Society
has done its part towards turning the mind of young
Belfast and young Ulster to that stirring record. It
took in hand the saving work of National Education,
and made it a success. Certain young men, some of
them connected with the *Morning News*, opened the
propaganda towards the end of 1883. They were but a
small band at first, their labours were little noticed at
the outset, they were afterwards censured in high
quarters as tending to wean some portion of the popular
forces from the national struggle. They stood to their
labours all the same with a real northern tenacity.
Their aim was to "spread the light" in the Ulster
capital, and make Irish literature as gracious a presence
in their neighbours' lives as it had proved in their
own. Several literary societies had failed in Belfast
before they arose ; a once promising association, the
Mangan Club, had just died. The weekly meetings
and lectures of the new society in St. Mary's Hall
showed, after some time, that more hopeful days might
be expected. On Mr. William McGrath, the first
secretary (now the Dublin Correspondent of the *Daily
News*), fell the lion's share of the organising. Gradually
the meetings attracted considerable attention, and gradually, too, the Society became a genuine factor in the
popular life of Belfast. The earliest workers included

Mr. J. P. Gaynor (now of the *Freeman's Journal*), Mr.
John McGrath (*United Ireland*), Mr. Simon O'Leary,
Mr. T. J. Hanna (*Irish News*), and others who now fill
prominent positions in London and the United States.
Like the Southwark lectures in London, the literary
and historical papers contributed to those Belfast meetings turned the minds of young Irishmen to new fields
and studies, and were a moulding influence in their lives.
The press soon began to give prominence to the work
of the Society, and Irish public men, Irish journalists
and Irish *littèrateurs* were attracted by its propaganda.
After Mr. McGrath, Mr. Gaynor, Mr. J. S. Murphy
and Mr. Hanna set their hands in succession to the
secretarial work, and had growing progress to report as
they left. In 1887, Mr. Jeremiah MacVeagh, now of
the London Irish Literary Society, and author of a
pamphlet (reprinted from the *Daily News*) on the Donegal
Land War, came in for this post. Mr. MacVeagh was
primarily a politician, though with strong literary
leanings. He was a born organiser, and under his care
the Society gave a new account of itself.

Mr. MacVeagh brought lecturers and speakers from
all parts of Ireland to his platform, men of standing and
repute in public life and in literature, and took care also
that the energies of the association should be always
active. Creeds and classes were united for literary
work and study under its auspices. Several of the
lectures (by Irish Members of Parliament, pressmen
and *littèrateurs*) have been reprinted from the local press
in pamphlet form, and the chief ones of the series would
afford a volume of vivid and racy Irish thought, research
and fancy. Nor was Irish music neglected here in the

BELFAST YOUNG IRELAND SOCIETY.

MICHAEL McCARTAN, M.P.

JEREMIAH MacVEAGH.

WILLIAM McGRATH.

J. P. GAYNOR.

JOSEPH DEVLIN

JOHN ROONEY.

heart of the North. Mr. MacVeagh resigned his post
in 1890, immediately before his removal to London.
Under his successor, Mr. Hanna, and the present secretary, Mr. Joseph Devlin, the record of success has gone
on. The presidents have included Mr. William Redmond, Mr. Sexton, M.P., and Mr. Michael McCartan,
M.P., who has held the post for the past six years.
A long page might be filled with the names of leading
Irishmen who have been identified in one way or
another with the work of the Society. Not the least
of its actions was the erection of a Celtic Cross over
the grave of Francis Davis, "The Belfast Man."
Altogether it may be fairly claimed that the Society has
organised and educated the young men of Belfast,
through the press its teachings have gone over Ulster, its
members have been kept in touch with the leading Irish
literary societies, and well in line with the present
forward movement. It has laid the basis of a fine force
in the new Ireland, for, as one of its workers justly
says, almost every member is a missionary of Young
Ireland principles.

Cork has a notable organisation in its Historical and
Archæological Society, which was founded in 1891. It
owes its origin to the (then) Very Rev. Canon R. A.
Sheehan, Vicar of SS. Peter and Paul's Church, in the
City of Cork, but since elevated to the episcopacy as
Bishop of Waterford and Lismore, in whose cathedral
city, the *Urbs Intacta*, he has this year (1894) founded the
Waterford and South-Eastern Counties Archæological
Society.* The objects of the Cork Society are " the

---

* His Lordship's inaugural address to this Society, delivered in
the Waterford City Hall, on January 24th, 1894, was a most interesting appeal for the study of Irish archæology, history, and kindred
subjects.

collection, preservation and diffusion of all available information regarding the past of the City and County of Cork," and also "to provide for the keeping of a record of local current events." To promote these objects meetings are held in the Library of the Crawford School of Art, Nile-street, Cork, mainly in the winter months, when papers on subjects coming under the above headings are read and discussed. The great work of the Society, may, however, be summed up in the publication of its *Journal*, the only monthly organ issued by any archæological society in the three kingdoms. Its first number came out in January, 1892, since when it has appeared regularly, and met with unstinted praise from all quarters, notably from the leading antiquarian authority in England, *The Antiquary*. It has a zealous roll of contributors, chief amongst them being H. W. Gillman, B.L., M.R.I.A., the writer of an able series of papers on the castles of the county; Robert Day, President (1894); H. L. Tivy; C. G. Doran (Queenstown), author of numerous poems; John O'Mahony, ex-Hon. Sec.; John Fitzgerald, "The Bard of the Lee;" J. P. Dalton, the present Hon. Secretary; H. F. Berry, M.A., T.C.D.; the Rev. Canon Courtenay Moore, M.A. (Mitchelstown); J. Grene Barry, J.P., M.R.S.A. (Limerick); T. Gleeson (Castlemartyr); Rev. P. Hurley, P.P. (Inchigeela); Denham Franklyn, J.P.; C. M. Tenison, M.R.S.A. (Tasmania); R. J. Ussher, J.P. (Ardmore); James Coleman, H.M.C., M.R.S.A.I. (Southampton); R. J. Lecky (London); Patrick Stanton; Rev. J. Lyons, P.P. (Macroom); Rev. Canon Brougham (Monkstown); J. P. Hayes; D. A. O'Leary (Charleville); Major J. Grove White, J. P. (Doneraile);

Thomas Crosbie (*Cork Examiner*), and G. M. Moore, M.R.S.A. I have given this long list of writers, for it is a most suggestive one. Fortunate indeed is the Irish county that can boast so varied an array of students and workers devoted to the preservation of its historical lore and its antiquarian riches. One thinks with a sense of pride and gratitude of the treasures that will be ready for the Munster historian after a few years, or a decade of such labours. Keen and sustained research, sympathetic and comprehensive study of the lights and monuments of the past characterise the whole system, for such it may be called. It is national education and national study of an ideal kind. Besides the several papers dealing with the celebrities, and the castles, abbeys and other antiquarian remains of the Co. Cork, and also the useful Notes and Queries section, a series of reprints of local poets' writings has also appeared in the *Journal ;* amongst them those of J. J. Callanan, Edward Walsh, Thomas Condon, as well as " The Monks of Kilcrea," by the late A. G. Geoghegan. Chapters of Smith's valuable History of Cork have accompanied every number of the *Journal* so far, enhanced and extended by learned notes from such Cork antiquaries as Crofton Croker and Dr. Caulfield. These notes are being carefully edited and expanded by Messrs. Robert Day and W. A. Copinger, B.L., LL.D., etc., the founder of the Bibliographical Society. The Cork Society's membership includes residents in North America, India and the Colonies. The sum total is not far from five hundred.

Amongst the most representative members of the Society, of some of whom portraits are given in this volume, I may mention the Most Rev. Dr. Sheehan, Bishop of Waterford and Lismore ; Mr. Robert Day, F.S.A., now President, who has long since achieved for himself the reputation of being one of the foremost archæologists in Ireland, and who is a frequent contributor to the Journal of the R.S.A.I., etc., as well as an enthusiastic collector of specimens of ancient Irish art, Irish antiquities, etc.; Mr. Denny Lane, M.A., one of the few survivors of the original *Nation* writers, and one who has identified himself with every movement calculated to benefit his native city, particularly in a literary or social direction ; Rev. Canon Courtenay Moore, editor of the *Irish Ecclesiastical Gazette,* author, amongst other works of an antiquarian character, of a remarkable pamphlet on *St. Patrick's Liturgy,* a broad-minded Protestant clergyman whose friendly relations with all sections of his countrymen furnish an admirable example that might be more widely followed up in Ireland; lastly, Mr. J. P. Dalton, the genial and devoted secretary, who besides being the author of several notable biographical and topographical sketches in the *Journal,*❋ is a frequent contributor of poetry to the Cork papers.

Certain Liverpool Irishmen have striven with great zeal during the past decade to accomplish a revival of Celtic ideas amongst their brethren and neighbours. Theirs is a most creditable record, telling of perseverance through depressing days. Liverpool or Lancashire generally cannot be called particularly literary, but most of the area is exceptionally interesting to the student of Irish thoughts and manners. Great

---

❋ *The Cork Historical and Archæological Journal* is published by Messrs. Guy & Co., at 70, Patrick Street, Cork.

novels are yet to be written of Irish life in Lancashire. Another Douglas Hyde might find within it as much Gaelic wealth to gather up as at home in the wild ways of Connaught. Some of the Irish element is far from being what we would wish it to be; but other sections of it are truly " kindly Irish of the Irish," rich in the old raciness. In the dreadful days of '47 and after, thousands of a once " bold peasantry " came hungry, hopeless, and despised to its shores, to a haunt of such gloom, hostility and bigotry as we find it difficult to picture in these tolerant and successful days. As they made their homes and raised their churches it might be said with little of a figure of speech that like the Jews after returning from captivity they had to build with one hand while the weapon of defence was ready in the other. The long struggle intensified their sturdy, tenacious Celtic spirit ; and they or their children to-day preserve in full vigour many traits that have become weakened with their brethren in other centres of Britain. A good deal of this Irish spirit is embodied in the members of the little circle which has struggled to propagate Irish intellectual ideas in Liverpool during the last ten years. They first of all started an Irish Literary Institute, which was formally inaugurated by Mr. Charles Dawson, M.P., in February, 1884. John Denvir was practically the founder of this body, and his son, Mr. J. M. Denvir, a capable journalist, was its first secretary. John Denvir's name is writ large through the history of the Irish in Liverpool, and indeed of Britain. He has taken part in the work of various Liverpool Irish literary clubs since 1850. He was connected at one time with the *Catholic Times,* and subse-

CORK HISTORICAL AND ARCHÆOLOGICAL SOCIETY

DENNY LANE.

ROBERT DAY.

THE MOST REV. DR. SHEEHAN.

CANON COURTENAY MOORE.

J. P. DALTON.

quently with the *United Irishman*, to both of which he contributed Irish verse and stories. In the eighties he conducted a paper, *The Nationalist*, for which members of the Southwark Club wrote largely. In earlier years he ran Denvir's Penny Irish Library—little volumes of Irish song, story, history, and drama (mainly original) which received regular enconiums from the popular press. The contributors included Dr. Commins, M.P., D. Crilly, M.P., F. J. Fox, John Hand, Hugh Heinrick, J. Lysaght Finegan, M.P., as well as Mr. Denvir and his son. Dr. Commins is one of the foremost Irish figures in Liverpool, is a clever lawyer, and a literary man of much culture and acumen. For the *Nation* and *United Irishman* some years ago he wrote lively verse, in which he satirised the "squireens" and the "crowbar brigades" of the time. He has translated continental poets, amongst them Freiligrath, whose sympathy with Irish aspiration was intense and constant. Returning to Mr. Denvir, we may note amongst his writing, "Rosaleen Dhu," and "The Gormans of Glenmore," two Irish plays, "The Reapers of Kilbride" and "The Brandons," two Irish serial tales. His chief work is, however, "The Irish in Britain," published two years ago ; a careful and sincere history, the labour of a man who knew every step of his ground. The Institute which he founded has had a strenuous career. Its lecturers went from time to time to most of the Irish centres of Lancashire and Yorkshire.

As in Southwark, "Original Nights" were tried, and proved fairly successful. The "Memorial Nights" were special features of the sessions, the celebration taking the form of papers, music and readings dealing

entirely with a poet or patriot (Davis, Mitchel, or such
another) as his anniversary came round. A great deal
was done from year to year towards creating a wide-
spread taste for Irish music and song. The leading
worker in the Institute (which last year became the
Liverpool Irish Literary Society) is a young Irishman
who deserves much more than a passing notice. Michael
O'Mahony is a dreamer of dreams, and much more as
we shall see. He was born some thirty years ago in
Bonmahon, a Waterford village, once the centre of the
Waterford copper mining district, and a sort of minia-
ture Tyre, as he says, but now the most unsightly
cluster of ruins in all Ireland. His father was a small
tenant farmer, small enough to be easily ruined.
O'Mahony came across to Swansea when he was about
seventeen years old. He read every book in its library,
and gathered enough of folk-lore from Gower, an
historic peninsula to the west of the town, inhabited
chiefly by descendants of Flemish invaders, to write
a story, "A Tale of Gower," which ran in the *Catholic
News*. In later days, and when he had removed to
Liverpool, he wrote a novel, "The Maid of Green-
church," dealing with the southern Tithe War. This
tale was immediately copied into the American press.
Several sketches, stories, and songs from his pen have
appeared in Munster papers. He is an authority on
Munster folk-lore, and a delightful *raconteur*. The fun,
spirit and drollery of Ireland in Lancashire he has
caught up with surprising ease and skill. Transferred
to printed pages they would be bracing literature. To
Celtic lore he adds Celtic eloquence, and these with
organising gifts, original views, and the quality of

initiative have made him a host in himself for the movement in Lancashire. He is a Catholic journalist, but we may confidently anticipate that his best work will be in the delineation of racy Irish life and character. Pioneers in Liverpool not yet noted are W. J. Ryan, once of the *Catholic News*, who is now scattering the seed of Irish ideas through Northumberland and Durham; Walter L. Cole, now of Dublin, J. Lalor, and John Morgan, artists who have exhibited Irish pictures at the well-known Liverpool Autumn Exhibitions; Father Power, now in Australia, once a contributor to the *Irish Fireside*, and a scholarly archæologist; Father Antoninus Byrne, also in Australia, author of Irish sketches, and poems in the *Month;* J. C. Quinn, B.Sc., one of the editors of the *Liverpool University Magazine;* J. H. Wolfe, now on the staff of *Fun;* W. F. Powell-Yates and Thomas Burke, whose forte is Irish lectures. In Mr. P. L. Beazley, a scholarly journalist, now editor of the *Catholic Times*, some readers will recognise an old contributor of Irish poems to the Dublin *Weekly News* and a translator of stories from continental languages. Mrs. Beazley wrote a good deal of poetry for the *Nation* some years ago over the signature " Nannie H. H.," and contributed Irish novels to *Young Ireland*.

Bradford Irishmen organised in August of last year an Irish Literary Society which already has given many signs of vigorous life. Mr. W. S. Burke and Mr. T. Loughlin, both enthusiasts in Irish literary matters laid the foundation of the scheme, gathered round themselves a circle of congenial spirits, and initiated a programme which was decidedly a new departure in Bradford. Their lines of study and work are similar to those of the

MICHAEL O'MAHONY.

London Society. Mr. Justin McCarthy, M.P., is the president, and in Mr. Councillor O'Flynn, chairman, the Society has secured one of the leading Irishmen in this important centre of Irish thought in Britain. The workers altogether are mainly young men, who have long been actively engaged in Irish organisations in Bradford. Mr. Loughlin who is secretary has taken his principles from Thomas Davis. Mr. James Gorman, another officer, is an active National Leaguer. Mr. Burke claims much more than a word. In his early home in Killaloe he was an eager student, whose thoughts turned to verse at a tender age. His first published efforts were in the *Weekly Freeman* of 1880 and 1881. From 1886 to 1890 he figured frequently in the pages of *United Ireland*. The *Dublin Journal*, a monthly started in 1887, found him a trusty supporter. He became assistant editor, and a contributor of verses, Irish scenic sketches and fiction. The *Journal* achieved good things, but through lack of capital and support it died at the end of a year. Subsequently, Mr. Burke worked for the Pan-Celtic Society. He wrote for the *Shamrock, Young Ireland, Evening Press, Weekly National Press*, and more recently contributed historical papers to the *Evening Telegraph*. He is now the managing editor of the Bradford *Catholic Herald*.

Last year, at the suggestion of the Rev. Denis O'Brien, who is justly regarded as the leader of the Irishmen of Bolton, Mr. William Devlin, the head-master of St. Mary's Schools in that town, began the work of organising the Bolton Irish Literary Society. Mr. Devlin was no stranger to such labours, for some time before he had established the Bolton Home Rule Literary

Society. The Irish forces in this Lancashire centre are
admirably organised, and this fact, added to the further
one that Mr. Devlin's heart was in the task, accounts
for the speedy success which attended his efforts.
Towards the close of the year, he delivered the inaugural lecture of the young society, taking for his subject
the Irish Parliament of 1689. Though only thirty-one
years of age, Mr. Devlin has a long roll of Irish and
educational work to his credit. Twelve years ago, fresh
from the highest honours in Hammersmith Training
College, he took the post of head-master at St. Mary's,
and long since secured more than a local reputation as
a successful teacher. He has been heard as a literary
and educational lecturer in leading towns of Lancashire.
In addition to Father O'Brien and Mr. Devlin, the
Bolton Society has active spirits in Mr. James Droogan,
Councillor Maginnis, Messrs. H. Kelly, R. Stewart, J.
Lawlor, G. Jones and J. Deighan.

Manchester also came into line last year. Mr. Daniel
Boyle, correspondent of the *Freeman* and National
League organiser, took the initiative and received the
support of several local Irish journalists : including Mr.
T. Scanlan, Mr. M. P. Lavelle, B.A., Mr. Cunningham,
Catholic Herald, and Mr. Gallagher, *Catholic Times*. Others
to rally early to the Society were Councillor McCabe,
J.P., Mr. J. Doran, J.P., Oldham, Mr. M. P. Ryan,
and Miss Mary Forrester. The inaugural lecture on
"Irish Music and Song," was delivered in February of
the present year by Mr. Alfred Perceval Graves. An
Irish class and a series of lectures on the Irish language
and literature were further items in the early programme.

In Bootle Mr. Henry Taaffe was the pioneer. For

many years he has been known in Bootle and Liverpool
as an Irish lecturer, and is a capital type of the quiet
organiser who full withal of earnestness and ideas
changes the local Irish element in the course of time
from a mass of units to a cohesive force.   Mr. Taaffe's
Irish literary training began years ago with John
Denvir's Irish Library.   The Irish Literary Society of
which he is president, though started only last year,
has already shown signs of vitality and vigour.   Bootle
has an imposing Irish force, and the helpers it has given
to Mr. Taaffe in his work are many.   Mr. E. McCann
is a zealous secretary.   Mr. Denis O'Brien entertains
the younger generation with curious stories of the
Liberator ; Mr. O'Connell McDonald and Mr. J. Davey
are men of '67 ; the Irish National Foresters are represented by Mr. John Quinn ; in Mr. J. G. Rowe, a very
young member of the Liverpool press, the Society has a
worker who gives promise of achieving distinction in the
field of Irish literature.   Though still in his teens he
has written voluminously, and Irish and other stories
from his pen have appeared in the *Shamrock* and in well-
known English papers.   Of certain periods of Irish
history he has made a special study, but is devoted above
all to literature.   Mr. J. J. Hayes was a contributor
some time back to the Scottish press.   Mr. James
Sexton is an authority on labour questions, and an
active figure in the labour world.   He is connected with
a few papers that cater for different sections of the
working classes, and writes labour novels with a purpose.

Going northward we find in Newcastle the East End
Irish Literary Society, founded last autumn.   The
inaugural lecture was delivered by Mr. W. J. Ryan, who

was, as we have seen, an old member of the Liverpool
Irish Literary Institute. As National League organiser in Northumberland and Durham Mr. Ryan has
been closely in touch with Irish masses in the north of
England. He has done yeoman service in the work of
popularising Irish literature and developing a taste for
systematic Irish reading throughout his area. He has
made Davis, Mitchel, and Boyle O'Reilly familiar and
loved in Irish colonies near and far from Tyneside. In
fact he has sought to accomplish an Irish revival of his
own in the North. He was on the press in Manchester
for some time, but I think he has found a more fruitful
Irish field. He is one of the " boys of Wexford," and
just twenty-nine years of age. Newcastle has also a
National Literary Association, amongst whose lecturers
is Mr. J. L. Garvan, of the *Newcastle Chronicle*, and
English Correspondent of *United Ireland*—a young Irishman of remarkable ability and enthusiasm. In Stockton
Mr. Daniel O'Keeffe is the pioneer.

The Dundee Catholic Literary Society, inaugurated
in June, 1893, by Mr. James J. Moran, is practically an
Irish literary society running on the usual lines. Mr.
Moran, who was born in Collooney, Co. Sligo, in July,
1872, has already fared far as a *littèrateur*. He began to
write for newspapers and magazines under various
pseudonyms at a very tender age. The first effort which
appeared with his name was a dramatic serial called
" Pat O'Neill's Vow," in *Young Ireland ;* a dramatised
version of which he is now preparing for the stage.
" The Dunferry Risin' : a tale of the I.R.B." ran later
on in the *Irish Emerald.* Last year his novel, " A
" Deformed Idol," appeared in book form, and won

praise from several critics. His humorous Irish stories in various periodicals he intends to publish under the title of "Irish Stew." From time to time he has devoted much attention to the early Irish writers of fiction. He is now the managing editor of the Dundee *Catholic Herald*.

In February, 1885, an Irish Literary Society was instituted in Glasgow by a number of young Irishmen eager to "spread the light." Messrs. James Johnston, P. A. Mooney, John Butler and John Rock were foremost in the band of the early promoters. Dr. Kevin Izod O'Doherty, ex-M.P., Wilfrid Blunt, Michael Davitt, Alfred Webb, Justin Huntly McCarthy and John Ferguson have held the office of honorary president of the Society. Messrs. Davitt, Webb and Ferguson have delivered their presidential addresses in the largest public halls in the city to audiences of more than three thousand persons. Well-known speakers have addressed large meetings on Irish literary questions from time to time under the auspices of the Society. The leading members of the association formed themselves in 1888 into the Glasgow Irish National Club, with the same objects in view as heretofore. The old success did not, however, crown their efforts under the new title. A short time ago, encouraged by the revival in Dublin and London they formed the present Society, which has adopted the old rules and objects. Several early members of the Society are now leading active journalistic careers : thus Mr. B. J. O'Neill is on the *Freeman's Journal*, Mr. P. A. Mooney is editing the *Donegal Independent*, Mr. P. J. Wilson is conducting the *Scottish Catholic*. Mr. John Ferguson is at present the honorary president,

while one of the first pioneers, Mr. James Johnson, dis-
charges the secretarial duties.

Although the Glasgow and West of Scotland Catholic
Literary Association has not adopted the word " Irish "
in its title, the membership is composed almost entirely
of Irish people, and one of its leading objects is the
encouragement of literature of an Irish character. The
first promoters were Frank Leslie, artist, P. A. Mooney,
whom we have just met, and Stephen J. Henry. The
association was inaugurated in October, 1890, at a meeting of influential Irish residents of Glasgow held in
Drummond's Hotel. The membership has increased so
steadily that for the past two years the weekly meetings
have had to be held in the City Hall Saloon. Excepting
His Grace the Archbishop of Glasgow, who is patron, the
organization is composed entirely of laymen. Not only
by their labours in the association, but by their regular
writings in the press, the members have wielded, and continue to wield much influence in the West of Scotland.

Sunderland has a small but a hard-working Irish
Literary Society, which originated in September, 1892.
Two types of the " Soggarth aroon " are at the head of
affairs here, for Father Smith is president, and Father
Murphy vice-president—he it was who delivered the
inaugural address on Thomas Davis. Papers on typical
Irish subjects are regularly rendered. Mr. T. Walsh is
secretary, and Mr. F. Molloy librarian. The Sunderland Society, by the way, is proud of its little Irish
library, the volumes of which circulate from home to
home, bearing the light of Celtic lore through what
the members regard as a benighted corner of England.

The Irish Society of East Anglia has a successful re-

cord. In August, 1890, Mr. A. Maunsell Atthill wrote
to the *Eastern Daily Press*, Norwich, suggesting the
formation of an Irish society, entirely non‐political,
wherein Irishmen living in the eastern counties of England might meet together sometimes on common ground.
This letter drew a cordial response from Mr. John
Keane, an Inland Revenue officer stationed at Norwich.
Mr. Atthill and Mr. Keane obtained a list of some
seventy Irishmen residing in East Anglia, and succeeded
in getting together a representative gathering on St.
Patrick's Day, 1891, when the Society was formally
constituted. Colonel H. H. A. Stewart, of Hopton
Hall, Norfolk, was elected president, and Mr. Keane
and Mr. Atthill joint secretaries. Other gentlemen who
rendered great assistance in the formation of the Society
were Dr. Charles O'Farrell and Mr. H. S. Meek, of
Great Yarmouth; and Messrs. E. D. Lowry and D.
W. Woods, of Norwich. The main objects of the
Society are the keeping fresh in the hearts of Irishmen
in Eastern England the memory of the old country, and
the relief as far as possible of the poorer class of their
fellow-countrymen. The president especially has done
much to keep the association in a flourishing condition.
Amongst the members, honorary or otherwise, are men
of such diverse views as the Cardinal Archbishop of
Armagh, the Marquis of Dufferin and Ava, Mr. Justin
McCarthy, Lord Ashbourne, Sir William McCormac,
Sir C. G. Duffy and Lord Roberts. Occasional concerts of Irish music take place, as well as meetings at
which papers on purely Irish subjects are read—those
by Mr. Keane, which are sometimes in Irish, taking a
notably high place.

Since October last Southampton has had its Irish Literary and Social Club, whose aim is to encourage Irish literature and develop the literary talents of the young Irishmen of Southampton. A monthly MS. magazine has been started, the contents to be articles, stories and poems, mainly Irish, by the members. The magazine bears the happy title of *The Leprechaun*, because, in the words of the member who suggested the name, "It shall be a little worker ; anyone who keeps it in sight will derive much good from it, and the name itself is distinctly Irish." Mr. P. J. Lawless, as the editor, will keep a special eye on *The Leprechaun.* The Club's president is Mr. P. Archer, and the secretary Mr. F. J. O'Mahony, both undoubted workers like *The Leprechaun* itself.

VIII.

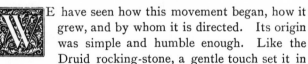E have seen how this movement began, how it grew, and by whom it is directed. Its origin was simple and humble enough. Like the Druid rocking-stone, a gentle touch set it in motion—a few young men made it possible. Their work, as it widened, touched that educational and literary instinct in the Irish nature which, however dormant or unnoted, is never wholly dead. The first workers were of that cultured and studious force in the Land League, who saw in the agitation at first a real national upheaval, a picturesque popular revolution, or who hoped to make it such, but who, as time went on, were somewhat disillusioned. Others came who had taken their lessons from Young Ireland, others who had looked deep into Celtic legend, others yet who had drunk at the old founts of Gaelic bardic poetry. Later still, the advisings of Sir Charles Gavan Duffy made an impression without as well as within the movement. The political strife of the past few years, which some believed would check or kill the revival, became in reality a strong source of help. Thoughtful Irish sec-

tions, aloof before, now paused and rallied to it. Here
was a national path, apart from odium and obloquy,
along which those who believed in Ireland could travel
with safety and with hope. Men of letters, whose pens
had been sold to an alien market, were attracted to it.
Irish students were taught how rich and gracious, if we
only see, is our Ireland of the past and of the present.
Some young Irishmen were taught how ignoble it was
that in their hours of leisure they should stand idly by
our street-corners, adding to the useless and clamorous
elements in Ireland, while foreign *savants* were pouring
with enthusiasm over our ancient manuscripts, while a
few devotees were gathering up the dying lore of Gaelic
Ireland, while a few, with seeing eyes, were declaring
that Ireland at heart was her old self, with vigour and
virility enough for a bright life yet amongst the nations.
The movement has not yet made new men of such
idlers, but it has caused some profitable searchings of
heart amongst the best of them.

We have noted that the movement is far from being
confined to Dublin or London. A weakness at present
is that there is little cohesion amongst its different bodies.
They have hardly a common programme ; they have
not a common organ. Literary Ireland is a thing of
many fragments, very far apart, and even yet very
strange to one another. Till they have a common
system, with a spirit of real brotherhood pervading them
all, some of the strength of this movement will be
wasted, will be spent in isolated or even in contrary
efforts.

It must be said of too many of the younger men who
ought to be its real strength that although their work

N

proves them to be stronger intellectually than their predecessors of Young Ireland, yet it is probable as things stand that in ten years they would not stir Ireland as effectually or render as noble an account of themselves as the Young Ireland coterie could in a twelvemonth. For many of them, able as they are, there is one thing needful before they can be forces as well as units. It is a missionary spirit. Irish sections here and there throughout Ireland and Great Britain now look up to them with hope, await their light and leading. Let them look to it that those who so watch and wait will not be in the smallest measure disappointed.

A nation that numbers amongst its younger school such writers as W. B. Yeats, William O'Brien, Miss Barlow, Standish O'Grady, T. W. Rolleston, Edmund Downey, Frank Mathew, Francis Fahy, Dr. Hyde, Katherine Tynan, Miss Sigerson, Miss Milligan and Lionel Johnson, stands in no need of ministering spirits. They and their brethren have been scattered so much, have worked in so many different channels, home and foreign, have mixed among, and been lost among so many foreign schools, that we have no idea of their number, their capacities till we slowly and patiently separate them from the crowd and call them to ourselves. It is our misfortune furthermore that in London and Boston, New York and Melbourne, writers of ours are "units merely of the undistinguished mass" of minor poets and novelists, who at home amid more congenial ways and audiences might be the delight of a nation. As Ireland grows more herself, more alive, more intellectual, the more will these misplaced children of song and story be drawn to her shores and her ideals.

To help towards so devoutly to be wished a consummation is another hope of our movement.

Certain it is that as the revival of Irish ideas grows apace, and the literary spirit blossoms into promising life in so many quarters, more cohesion, more fraternity, more of a missionary spirit are amongst our needs, in order that the two great objects of the movement—influence as an educating and teaching force, and literary creativeness—may go on and widen. In the educational direction we can all labour, continuing and perfecting the work which will be handed over at a future day to a real National Board of Education. We can carry out Sir Gavan Duffy's wise purpose and desire of bringing technical lore to our peasants, showing them the riches of the soil, the homely world about them. They will learn that true nationhood presupposes a people thoroughly conversant with their own characteristics and powers, keenly conscious of their industrial and other resources, proud of their rights and their home institutions, manly, dignified, self-supporting, but in sympathy with the human and spiritual interests of outer humanity; loving their own artistic and intellectual creations, and finding in them something spiritually noble to rally to ; distinctive but not insular. As yet, the unfortunate truth is that three-fourths of our people are as strangers in their own land ; strangers to her capacities, strangers to her traditions and her proudest associations. There is an appealing legend of ours which tells that in a cave under Aileach, in Donegal, a band of the old Fenian heroes lie sleeping through the ages, awaiting the day of Ireland's successful uprising for independence, when they will

come forth to take their places in the ranks beside
their living kindred. Dim and mysterious as these
forms in the gloom of the mountain cave appear to our
minds are too many of the first figures of Irish history
even yet. They are apart, unreal, or all but lost—theirs
is a legend-life at the best. Yet in a vivid-living, a
studious, a creative Ireland, the dramatist, the artist,
the ballad-writer, would find material for their live's
best work in those heroes and those ways we have allowed
to grow dim. The study would vivify our national
life. As for our legendary riches and our little-known
Gaelic fields, they are fascinating. Fine work has been
done of late years for Irish folk-lore, but higher matters
of Irish mythology are, strangely enough, neglected.
We have taken our notions of the old gods from peasant
stories; we have, as it were, surveyed the Irish Olympus
through cabin-smoke. Some of us, perhaps, never gave
it a glance or a thought. To many, with whom Jove
and Diana and Pan are abiding figures, Dagda Mor and
Mananan are the merest shadows. Afar in the western
ocean in the bygone ages the Celtic fancy saw the
beautiful islands of light and youth. There the gods
and the great spirits had abode. Time and sorrow were
strangers by those mystic waves in the West. There
Oisin sang of the Fenii; there Mananan, the great god
of the sea, had his home; there the three queen-sisters—
Eire, Fohla, and Banba—lived in immortal peace.
There were the mystic bell-branches, which to all who
listened brought glorious sleep under the enchanted
trees. In fine, the lore of that western world is almost
an epic in itself, and one which in these days, when so
much materialism invades us from the East, it were well

we studied somewhat more than we do. Immortal itself,
as the old bards deemed, it might be also the instrument
of immortality to many an Irish writer. We must try
to make it familar by Irish firesides.

As the Irish revival expands in new directions, will
not some one take heart and attempt something for
Irish dramatic literature? The real Irish drama is a
thing unknown. Why it is so is to me something of a
marvel; for in our tastes, ideas, and lives we are
essentially dramatic. And surely the materials for the
national drama are wasting in profusion before us. We
may see in our day in Dublin genuine Irish plays, of
truth and talent, written for the people, prized by the
people, moving and moulding the people. Otherwise I
fear that the city will not half deserve to be the capital
of a nation.

Leaving the question of the revival of Irish ideas
generally, which every day becomes more palpable and
hopeful, and examining the possibility which is the most
important of all—the possibility of a new, characteristic,
and original Irish literature—there are signs that thrill
and cheer. Our writers, for one thing, are becoming
more sensible of the dignity of literature, more devoted
to it for its own sake. With some of their forerunners
literature was now and then a spasmodic or half-hearted
affair, neither an art nor a passion nor even a great
pursuit. They stood within the sanctuary, but gave no
sign which told that they had the sacred " vocation."
Now a higher order of things is arising. Life, humanity,
imagination, are taking the place of polemics and
abstractions in Irish prose and verse.

Our writers will not want materials after their own

hearts. Some there are who will find their highest inspiration in their own inner lives; others will seek it in the complex, strenuous life of our new Ireland. Others in the olden legends, stories, life-ways, will have fresh and fruitful ground, as yet only partially broken. Leaving England, where so much of latter-day thought and song is suggestive of decay, decrepitude and dying impulse, and landing on Celtic shores, is like passing from a worn old world to the rich vistas and the exultant life of a new, to feel

> " Like stout Cortez, when with eagle eyes
> He stared at the Pacific, and all his men
> Looked at each other with a wild surmise,
> Silent, upon a peak in Darien."

So much are these possibilities being taken advantage of that a critic recently declared that latter-day English literature is fast becoming an Irish literature. In the most eloquent words that Sir Gavan Duffy used of late years he expressed the conviction that in Ireland " there is place for a great experiment for humanity." Perhaps it can be said, with even greater truth, that in Ireland there is place for a great experiment for literature.

As the leading writers sketched in preceding pages gave us their typical books—Standish O'Grady, William O'Brien, W. B. Yeats, and the rest—had not each book an interest outside and beyond itself? Was it not as a light rising out of a dark country, showing us charms and possibilities of which we had been entirely oblivious ? " Spread the Light "—such light as this—we well may say to these writers. And well may we advise our younger authors to seek that dark country of charms and beauties unexplored.

We will aim to promote in new quarters that enlightened nationality which studies the past, prizes the best in it, keeps it as a meet background to lives of noble action in the present; whose intelligent aim through the years is the development of all that is worthy and distinctive in the nation. Ireland's best will never have a fair field until a great system of National Education, framed on a Celtic basis, meeting at every turn the requirements and characteristics of the people, has had time to become, as it were, part and parcel of the nation. Our movement is doing something to supply the want; and there are splendid possibilities before it in the same direction. When it has found an organ or a press of its own, the course will be surer. Meanwhile, and after, our authors, with their more subtle graces, will be drawing brighter native ideals around the masses. They will illustrate life after our own hearts, and bring more hallowed associations around our Irish scenery. They will, if true to their genius, create characters that will enrich our lives, that will touch our Celtic sympathies, stir our latent or living worthiness; characters to which we will rally, and be the better men and women for so doing.

Such then is the movement—literary in essence, social and national in some of its purposes and effects. Its aim is to teach Ireland to see herself, to be herself, to set her in her true place, realising her nature and her mission. It is an effort to bring knowledge, books, brave hopes, Celtic idealism as her ministering spirits. Its pioneers have it in their power to touch, to thrill, to weld together for the noblest national purposes all that is thoughtful, strenuous, and original in their own land.

R2

But their mission must not be a mere transient, recreative, after-dinner idea—it must be a constant plan and passion. Most interesting of all are the efforts of the *littèrateurs* in the heart of the movement. Should they tend, as they promise, to keener interpretation than hitherto of Ireland's life, to brighter developments of Ireland's genius, the gain will be not only hers but humanity's.

THE END

PATERNOSTER STEAM PRESS, IVY LANE, LONDON; AND FROME.